The Anti-Inflammatory Slow Cooker Cookbook: 250 Easy Flavorful Recipes for Balanced Meals and Healthy Living

Diana Parker

Disclaimer:

All information and resources found in this book are based on
the opinions of the author. All information is intended to
motivate readers to make their own health, nutrition, and fitness
decisions after consulting with their health care provider. The
macro plans are not medically-prescribed diets. The focus is
meal prep education and recipe ideas.

We encourage you to consult a doctor before making any health
or diet changes, especially any changes related to a specific
diagnosis or condition. NO information in this book should be
used to diagnose, treat, prevent, or cure any disease or condition

CONTENTS

Breakfast Recipes
Carrot Oatmeal

Preparation time: 10 minutes
Cooking time: 8 hours
Servings: 4

Ingredients:
- ½ cup oatmeal
- 1 carrot, grated
- 1 ½ cups coconut milk
- ¼ zucchini, grated
- ½ teaspoon cinnamon
- 2 tablespoons honey
- ¼ cup pecans, chopped

Directions:
1. In your Slow cooker, mix oats with carrot, coconut milk, zucchini, cloves, nutmeg, cinnamon, and honey, stir, cover, and cook on Low for 8 hours.
2. Add pecans, toss, divide into bowls and serve.

per serving: 360 calories,4.9g protein, 24.2g carbohydrates, 29.7g fat, 4.8g fiber, 0mg cholesterol, 26mg sodium, 405mg potassium.

Honey Toast

Preparation time: 10 minutes
Cooking time: 4 hours
Servings: 4

Ingredients:
- Cooking spray
- 4 slices of multigrain bread
- 1 tablespoon honey
- 3 eggs
- 1 ½ cups coconut milk
- 1 teaspoon vanilla extract
- 1 oz dark chocolate
- 1 teaspoon ground cinnamon

Directions:
1. Grease your Slow cooker with the cooking spray and arrange bread cubes inside.
2. In a bowl, mix the eggs with coconut milk, honey, vanilla, cinnamon, and chocolate chips, whisk well, add to the slow cooker, cover and cook on Low for 4 hours.
3. Divide into bowls and serve for breakfast.

per serving: 381 calories,10.3g protein, 25.7g carbohydrates, 28g fat, 4.5g fiber, 124mg cholesterol, 175mg sodium, 374mg potassium.

Cinnamon Rice

Preparation time: 10 minutes
Cooking time: 7 hours
Servings: 9

Ingredients:

- 4 apples, cored, peeled, and chopped
- 2 tablespoons coconut oil
- 2 teaspoons cinnamon
- 1 ½ cups brown rice
- ½ teaspoon vanilla extract
- ¼ teaspoon ground nutmeg
- 5 cups of coconut milk

Directions:

1. In the Slow cooker, put apples, cinnamon, rice, vanilla, nutmeg, and coconut milk, cover, cook on Low for 7 hours, stir, divide into bowls and serve for breakfast.

per serving: 501 calories,5.7g protein, 45.7g carbohydrates, 35.9g fat, 6.7g fiber, 0mg cholesterol, 22mg sodium, 5mg potassium.

Sweet Mix

Preparation time: 10 minutes
Cooking time: 6 hours
Servings: 8

Ingredients:

- 2 cups quinoa
- 2 bananas, mashed
- 4 cups of water
- 2 cups blueberries
- 2 teaspoons vanilla extract
- 2 tablespoons honey
- 1 teaspoon ground cinnamon
- Cooking spray

Directions:

1. Grease your Slow cooker with cooking spray, add quinoa, bananas, water, blueberries, vanilla, maple syrup, and cinnamon, stir, cover, and cook on Low for 6 hours.
2. Stir again, divide into bowls and serve for breakfast.

per serving: 223 calories,6.6g protein, 44g carbohydrates,2.8g fat, 4.8g fiber, 0mg cholesterol, 7mg sodium, 380mg potassium.

Vanilla Quinoa

Preparation time: 10 minutes
Cooking time: 4 hours
Servings: 4

Ingredients:
- 1 cup quinoa
- 2 cups of coconut milk
- 2 cups of water
- ¼ cup stevia
- 1 teaspoon ground cinnamon
- 1 teaspoon vanilla extract

Directions:
1. In your Slow cooker, mix quinoa with milk, water, stevia, cinnamon, and vanilla, stir, cover, cook on Low for 3 hours and 30 minutes, stir, cook for 30 minutes more, divide into bowls, and serve for breakfast.

per serving: 437 calories,8.8g protein, 34.5g carbohydrates, 31.2g fat, 5.9g fiber, 0mg cholesterol, 24mg sodium, 560mg potassium.

Nuts Quinoa

Preparation time: 10 minutes
Cooking time: 10 hours
Servings: 6

Ingredients:
- ¾ cup quinoa
- ¾ cup oatmeal
- 2 tablespoons honey
- 1 cup apricots, chopped
- 6 cups of water
- 1 teaspoon vanilla extract
- ¾ cup hazelnuts, chopped

Directions:
1. In your Slow cooker, mix quinoa with oats honey, apricots, water, vanilla, and hazelnuts, stir, cover, and cook on Low for 10 hours.
2. Stir quinoa mix again divides into bowls, and serve for breakfast.

per serving: 212 calories,6.1g protein, 30.8g carbohydrates, 7.8g fat, 3.9g fiber, 0mg cholesterol, 10mg sodium, 294mg potassium.

Flaxseeds Oatmeal

Preparation time: 10 minutes
Cooking time: 8 hours
Servings: 4

Ingredients:

- ½ cup quinoa
- 1 cup oatmeals
- 1 teaspoon vanilla extract
- 5 cups of water
- Zest of 1 lemon, grated
- 1 teaspoon vanilla extract
- 2 tablespoons flaxseed
- 1 tablespoon coconut oil
- 3 tablespoons honey
- 1 cup blueberries

Directions:

1. In your Slow cooker, mix quinoa, water, oats, vanilla, lemon zest, flaxseed, honey, and blueberries, stir, cover, and cook on Low for 8 hours.
2. Divide into bowls and serve for breakfast.

per serving: 275 calories,6.7g protein, 46.8g carbohydrates, 7.3g fat, 5.4g fiber, 0mg cholesterol, 13mg sodium, 263mg potassium.

Coconut Bake

Preparation time: 10 minutes
Cooking time: 7 hours
Servings: 5

Ingredients:

- 1 cup quinoa
- 4 tablespoons olive oil
- 2 cups of water
- ½ cup dates, chopped
- 3 bananas, chopped
- ¼ cup coconut, shredded
- 2 teaspoons ground cinnamon
- 2 tablespoons honey
- 1 cup walnuts, toasted and chopped

Directions:

1. Put the oil in your Slow cooker, add quinoa, water, dates, bananas, coconut, cinnamon, honey, and walnuts, stir, cover, and cook on Low for 7 hours.
2. Divide into bowls and serve for breakfast.

per serving: 531 calories,12.2g protein, 62.1g carbohydrates, 29.7g fat,8.2g fiber, 0mg cholesterol, 7mg sodium, 716mg potassium.

Oregano Mix

Preparation time: 10 minutes
Cooking time: 8 hours
Servings: 6

Ingredients:

- 3 garlic cloves, minced
- 1 yellow onion, chopped
- 1 celery stalk, chopped
- 2 red bell peppers, chopped
- 12 ounces canned tomatoes, chopped
- 4 cups vegetable stock
- 1 cup lentils
- 14 ounces pinto beans
- 2 tablespoons chili powder
- ½ cup quinoa
- 1 tablespoons oregano, chopped
- 2 teaspoon cumin, ground

Directions:

1. In your Slow cooker, mix garlic with the onion, celery, bell peppers, tomatoes, stock, lentils, pinto beans, chili powder, quinoa, oregano, and cumin, stir, cover, cook on Low for 8 hours, divide between plates and serve for breakfast

per serving: 444 calories, 26.4g protein, 80g carbohydrates, 3g fat, 24.3g fiber, 0mg cholesterol, 78mg sodium, 1629mg potassium.

Coconut Pudding

Preparation time: 10 minutes
Cooking time: 1 hour and 30 minutes
Servings: 4

Ingredients:

- 3 egg yolks
- 6 ounces coconut cream
- 1 teaspoon vanilla extract
- 2 tablespoons honey

Directions:

1. In a bowl, mix the egg yolks with honey and whisk well.
2. Add Greek-style yogurt and vanilla extract, whisk well, pour into your 4 ramekins, place them in your Slow cooker, add some water to the slow cooker, cover and cook on High for 1 hour and 30 minutes.
3. Leave aside to cool down and serve.

per serving: 173 calories, 3g protein, 11.6g carbohydrates, 13.5g fat, 1g fiber, 157mg cholesterol, 13mg sodium, 133mg potassium.

Curry Quinoa

Preparation time: 10 minutes
Cooking time: 6 hours
Servings: 6

Ingredients:

- 1 yellow onion, chopped
- 1 tablespoon olive oil
- 3 garlic cloves, minced
- 2 teaspoons oregano, dried
- 1 ½ pound chicken breasts, skinless, boneless, and chopped
- 2 teaspoons parsley, dried
- 2 teaspoons curry powder
- ½ teaspoon chili flakes
- 1 butternut squash, peeled and cubed
- 2/3 cup quinoa
- 12 ounces canned tomatoes, chopped
- 4 cups vegetable stock

Directions:

1. In your Slow cooker, mix the onion with oil, garlic, oregano, chicken, parsley, curry powder, chili, squash, quinoa, tomatoes, and stock, stir, cover, and cook on Low for 6 hours.
2. Divide into bowls and serve for breakfast.

per serving: 343 calories, 36.9g protein, 20.6g carbohydrates, 12.2g fat, 3.7g fiber, 101mg cholesterol, 137mg sodium, 653mg potassium.

Chia Seeds Mix

Preparation time: 10 minutes
Cooking time: 8 hours
Servings: 4

Ingredients:

- 1 cup oatmeal
- 1 cup of water
- 3 cups organic almond milk
- 2 tablespoons chia seeds
- ¼ cup pomegranate seeds
- ¼ cup dried blueberries
- ¼ cup almonds, sliced

Directions:

1. In your Slow cooker, mix oats with water, organic almond milk, chia seeds, pomegranate ones, blueberries, and almonds, stir, cover, and cook on Low for 8 hours.
2. Stir again, divide into bowls and serve for breakfast.

per serving: 173 calories, 5.5g protein, 22.9g carbohydrates, 7.1g fat, 5.8g fiber, 0mg cholesterol, 42mg sodium, 199mg potassium.

Parmesan Breakfast

Preparation time: 10 minutes
Cooking time: 3 hours
Servings: 4

Ingredients:
- 1-pound chicken breasts, skinless, boneless, and cubed
- ½ teaspoon basil, dried
- ¾ cup flaxseed, ground
- ¼ cup chia seeds
- ¼ cup parmesan, grated
- ½ teaspoon oregano, chopped
- 2 eggs
- 2 garlic cloves, minced

Directions:
1. In a bowl, mix flaxseed with chia seeds, parmesan, pepper, oregano, garlic, and basil and stir.
2. Put the eggs in a second bowl and whisk them well.
3. Dip chicken in eggs mix, then in chia seeds mix, put them in your Slow cooker after you've greased it with cooking spray, cover, and cook on High for 3 hours.
4. Serve them right away for a Sunday breakfast.

per serving: 475 calories,46.4g protein, 13.3g carbohydrates, 24.6g fat, 10.7g fiber, 193mg cholesterol, 267mg sodium, 543mg potassium.

Coffee Latte Mix

Preparation time: 10 minutes
Cooking time: 6 hours
Servings: 4

Ingredients:
- 1 cup hot coffee
- 1 cup quinoa
- 1 cup of coconut water
- 2 oz dark chocolate
- ½ cup coconut cream

Directions:
1. In your Slow cooker, mix quinoa with coffee, coconut water, and chocolate chips, cover, and cook on Low for 6 hours.
2. Stir, divide into bowls, spread coconut cream all over, and serve for breakfast.

per serving: 313 calories,8.3g protein, 39.6g carbohydrates, 14.1g fat, 4.8g fiber, 3mg cholesterol, 82mg sodium, 550mg potassium.

Nutmeg Quinoa

Preparation time: 10 minutes
Cooking time: 6 hours
Servings: 6

Ingredients:
- 1 cup quinoa
- 1 egg white
- 2 cups of coconut milk
- ¼ teaspoon vanilla extract
- 1 tablespoon honey
- ¼ teaspoon cardamom, ground
- ¼ teaspoon ginger, grated
- ¼ teaspoon ground cinnamon
- ¼ teaspoon vanilla extract
- ¼ teaspoon nutmeg, ground
- 1 tablespoon coconut flakes

Directions:
1. In your Slow cooker, mix quinoa with egg white, milk, vanilla, honey, cardamom, ginger, cinnamon, vanilla, and nutmeg, stir a bit, cover and cook on Low for 6 hours.
2. Stir, divide into bowls, and serve for breakfast with coconut flakes on top.

per serving: 307 calories,6.5g protein, 25.9g carbohydrates, 21.1g fat, 5.2g fiber, 0mg cholesterol, 19mg sodium, 387mg potassium.

Almond Pudding

Preparation time: 10 minutes
Cooking time: 2 hours
Servings: 2

Ingredients:
- ¼ cup honey
- 3 cups organic almond milk
- 1 cup cauliflower rice
- 2 tablespoons vanilla extract

Directions:
1. Put cauliflower rice in your Slow cooker, add maple syrup, organic almond milk, and vanilla extract, stir, cover, and cook on High for 2 hours.
2. Stir your pudding again, divide into bowls and serve for breakfast.

per serving: 224 calories,2.6g protein, 43.9g carbohydrates, 2.2g fat, 0.6g fiber, 0mg cholesterol, 138mg sodium, 131mg potassium.

Lemon Pudding

Preparation time: 10 minutes
Cooking time: 1 hour and 40 minutes
Servings: 6

Ingredients:

- 2 oz coconut oil
- 2 ounces honey
- 7 ounces almond flour
- ½ cup of coconut milk
- 1 teaspoon vanilla extract
- Zest of ½ lemon, grated
- Cooking spray
- 1 egg

Directions:

1. In a bowl, mix honey, milk, vanilla, lemon zest, and eggs and whisk well.
2. Add flour and whisk well again.
3. Grease your Slow cooker with cooking spray, add pudding mix, spread, cover, and cook on High for 1 hour and 30 minutes.
4. Divide between plates and serve for breakfast.

per serving: 301 calories,6.1g protein, 13.8g carbohydrates, 25.4g fat, 2.8g fiber, 27mg cholesterol, 22mg sodium, 68mg potassium.

Chicken Casserole

Preparation time: 10 minutes
Cooking time: 8 hours
Servings: 4

Ingredients:

- 8 eggs, whisked
- 1 yellow onion, chopped
- 1-pound chicken sausages, homemade
- 2 teaspoons basil, dried
- 1 tablespoon garlic powder
- 1 yellow bell pepper, chopped
- 1 teaspoon olive oil

Directions:

1. Grease your Slow cooker with olive oil, add eggs, onion, beef sausage, basil, garlic powder, pepper, and yellow bell pepper, toss, cover, and cook on Low for 8 hours.
2. Slice, divide between plates, and serve for breakfast.

per serving: 378 calories,26.8g protein, 14.6g carbohydrates, 22.5g fat, 1.9g fiber, 327mg cholesterol, 579mg sodium, 238mg potassium.

Sweet Paprika Casserole

Preparation time: 10 minutes
Cooking time: 4 hours
Servings: 8

Ingredients:

- 8 eggs
- 4 egg whites
- 2 teaspoons mustard
- ¾ cup of organic almond milk
- 2 red bell peppers, chopped
- 1 yellow onion, chopped
- 1 teaspoon sweet paprika
- 6 oz tofu, crumbled
- Cooking spray

Directions:

1. In a bowl, mix the eggs with egg whites, mustard, milk, and sweet paprika and whisk well.
2. Grease your Slow cooker with cooking spray and spread bell peppers, bacon, and onion on the bottom.
3. Add mixed eggs, sprinkle tofu all over, cover, and cook on Low for 4 hours.
4. Divide between plates and serve for breakfast.

per serving: 158 calories,10.3g protein, 6g carbohydrates, 11g fat, 1.6g fiber, 164mg cholesterol, 86mg sodium, 264mg potassium.

Chicken Frittata

Preparation time: 10 minutes
Cooking time: 3 hours
Servings: 2

Ingredients:

- ½ cup chicken, cooked and shredded
- 1 teaspoon mustard
- 1 tomato, chopped
- 4 eggs
- 1 small avocado, pitted, peeled, and chopped

Directions:

1. In a bowl, mix the eggs with chicken, avocado, tomato, and mustard, toss, transfer to your Slow cooker, cover and cook on Low for 3 hours.
2. Divide between plates and serve for breakfast

per serving: 397 calories,23.8g protein, 11.1g carbohydrates, 29.9g fat, 7.3g fiber, 354mg cholesterol, 153mg sodium, 756mg potassium.

Goat Cheese Breakfast

Preparation time: 10 minutes
Cooking time: 4 hours
Servings: 4

Ingredients:
- 8 eggs, beaten
- ½ cup of coconut milk
- 1 teaspoon oregano, dried
- 4 cups baby arugula
- 1 and ¼ cup roasted red peppers, chopped
- ½ cup red onion, chopped
- ¾ cup goat cheese, crumbled
- Cooking spray

Directions:
1. In a bowl, mix the eggs with milk, oregano, and whisk well.
2. Grease your Slow cooker with cooking spray and spread roasted peppers, onion and arugula.
3. Add eggs mix, sprinkle goat cheese all over, cover, cook on Low for 4 hours, divide frittata between plates and serve for breakfast.

per serving: 246 calories,14.6g protein, 8.3g carbohydrates, 18.1g fat, 2.1g fiber, 333mg cholesterol, 289mg sodium, 396mg potassium.

Sausage and Eggs Scramble

Preparation time: 10 minutes
Cooking time: 6 hours
Servings: 6

Ingredients:
- 12 eggs
- 14 oz chicken sausages, homemade
- 1 cup of coconut milk
- 16 ounces tofu
- 1 teaspoon basil, dried
- 1 teaspoon oregano, dried
- Cooking spray

Directions:
1. Grease your Slow cooker with cooking spray, spread sausages on the bottom, crack eggs, add milk, basil, oregano, whisk a bit, sprinkle tofu all over, cover, and cook on Low for 6 hours.
2. Divide egg and sausage scramble between plates and serve.

per serving: 297 calories,26.8g protein, 8.8g carbohydrates, 28.8g fat, 2.1g fiber, 327mg cholesterol, 403mg sodium, 340mg potassium.

Kale Omelet

Preparation time: 10 minutes
Cooking time: 3 hours
Servings: 4

Ingredients:

- 1 teaspoon olive oil
- 7 ounces roasted red peppers, chopped
- 6 ounces baby kale
- 6 ounces feta cheese, crumbled
- ¼ cup green onions, sliced
- 7 eggs, whisked

Directions:

1. In a bowl, mix the eggs with cheese, kale, red peppers, green onions, whisk well, pour into the Slow cooker after you've greased it with the oil, cover, cook on Low for 3 hours, divide between plates, and serve right away.

per serving: 270 calories,17.8g protein, 10.3g carbohydrates, 18.2g fat, 1.8g fiber, 324mg cholesterol, 719mg sodium, 229mg potassium.

Seafood Frittata

Preparation time: 10 minutes
Cooking time: 3 hours and 40 minutes
Servings: 3

Ingredients:

- 4 eggs, whisked
- ½ teaspoon olive oil
- 2 tablespoons green onions, chopped
- 4 ounces salmon, chopped, cooked

Directions:

1. Drizzle the oil in your Slow cooker, add eggs, whisk, cover, and cook on Low for 3 hours.
2. Add salmon and green onions, toss a bit, cover, cook on Low for 40 minutes more, and divide between plates.
3. Serve right away for breakfast.

per serving: 142 calories,14.8g protein, 0.7g carbohydrates, 8.9g fat, 0.1g fiber, 235mg cholesterol, 99mg sodium, 14.8mg potassium.

Sweet Cardamom Bowls

Preparation time: 5 minutes
Cooking time: 3 hours
Servings: 5

Ingredients:

- 1 teaspoon ground cinnamon
- ½ teaspoon nutmeg, ground
- ½ cup almonds, chopped
- 1 teaspoon honey
- 1.5 cup of coconut milk
- ¼ teaspoon cardamom, ground
- ¼ teaspoon cloves, ground

Directions:

1. In your Slow cooker, mix the coconut milk with cinnamon, nutmeg, almonds, honey, cardamom, and cloves, stir, cover, cook on Low for 3 hours, divide into bowls and serve for breakfast

per serving: 228 calories, 3.7g protein, 7.8g carbohydrates, 22g fat, 3.1g fiber, 0mg cholesterol, 11mg sodium, 265mg potassium.

Brussels Sprouts Omelet

Preparation time: 10 minutes
Cooking time: 4 hours
Servings: 4

Ingredients:

- 4 eggs, whisked
- 1 tablespoon olive oil
- 2 green onions, minced
- 2 garlic cloves, minced
- 12 ounces Brussels sprouts, sliced

Directions:

1. Drizzle the oil on the bottom of your Slow cooker and spread Brussels sprouts, garlic, green onions, eggs, toss, cover, and cook on Low for 4 hours.
2. Divide between plates and serve right away for breakfast.

per serving: 134 calories, 8.7g protein, 9.1g carbohydrates, 8.2g fat, 3.4g fiber, 164mg cholesterol, 84mg sodium, 416mg potassium.

Mushrooms Casserole

Preparation time: 10 minutes
Cooking time: 4 hours
Servings: 4

Ingredients:

- 1 teaspoon lemon zest, grated
- 10 ounces goat cheese, cubed
- 1 tablespoon lemon juice
- 1 tablespoon apple cider vinegar
- 1 tablespoon olive oil
- 2 garlic cloves, minced
- 10 ounces spinach, torn
- ½ cup yellow onion, chopped
- ½ teaspoon basil, dried
- 8 ounces mushrooms, sliced
- Cooking spray

Directions:

1. Spray your Slow cooker with cooking spray, arrange cheese cubes on the bottom and add lemon zest, lemon juice, vinegar, olive oil, garlic, spinach, onion, basil, mushrooms.
2. Toss well, cover, cook on Low for 4 hours, divide between plates and serve for breakfast right away.

per serving: 389 calories,25.7g protein, 8g carbohydrates, 29.2g fat, 2.5g fiber, 74mg cholesterol, 306mg sodium, 646mg potassium.

Vanilla Oatmeal

Preparation time: 10 minutes
Cooking time: 6 hours
Servings: 2

Ingredients:

- 1 cup organic almond milk
- ½ cup oatmeal
- ½ cup cranberries
- ½ teaspoon vanilla extract
- 1 tablespoon honey

Directions:

1. In your slow cooker, mix the oats with the berries, milk, and the other ingredients, toss, put the lid on and cook on Low for 6 hours.
2. Divide into bowls and serve for breakfast.

per serving: 157 calories,3.2g protein, 29.1g carbohydrates, 2.6g fat, 3.6g fiber, 0mg cholesterol, 77mg sodium, 218mg potassium.

Coconut Milk Pudding

Preparation time: 10 minutes
Cooking time: 8 hours
Servings: 4

Ingredients:
- 4 carrots, grated
- 1 ½ cups coconut milk
- ½ teaspoon ground cinnamon
- 2 tablespoons honey
- ¼ cup walnuts, chopped
- 1 teaspoon vanilla extract

Directions:
1. In your Slow cooker, mix carrots with milk, cloves, nutmeg, cinnamon, honey, walnuts, and vanilla extract, stir, cover, and cook on Low for 8 hours.
2. Divide into bowls and serve for breakfast.

per serving: 313 calories,4.5g protein, 20.6g carbohydrates, 26.1g fat, 4.2g fiber, 0mg cholesterol, 56mg sodium, 479mg potassium.

Eggs Casserole

Preparation time: 10 minutes
Cooking time: 5 hours
Servings: 2

Ingredients:
- ½ cup mozzarella, shredded
- 2 eggs, whisked
- ½ tablespoon balsamic vinegar
- ½ tablespoon olive oil
- 4 ounces' baby kale
- 1 red onion, chopped
- ¼ teaspoon oregano
- ½ pound white mushrooms, sliced
- Cooking spray

Directions:
1. In a bowl, mix the eggs with the kale, mushrooms, and the other ingredients except for the cheese and cooking spray and stir well.
2. Grease your slow cooker with cooking spray, add the mushroom mix, spread, sprinkle the mozzarella all over, put the lid on, and cook on Low for 5 hours.
3. Divide between plates and serve for breakfast.

per serving: 206 calories,14.7g protein, 18.6g carbohydrates, 10g fat, 4.4g fiber, 167mg cholesterol, 148mg sodium, 506mg potassium.

Cardamom Apple Bowls

Preparation time: 10 minutes
Cooking time: 6 hours
Servings: 3

Ingredients:

- 2 apples, cored, peeled, and cut into medium chunks
- 1 tablespoon honey
- 1 tablespoon ginger, grated
- 1 cup of coconut milk
- ¼ teaspoon ground cinnamon
- ½ teaspoon vanilla extract
- ¼ teaspoon cardamom, ground

Directions:

1. In your slow cooker, combine the apples with the honey, ginger, and the other ingredients, toss, put the lid on, and cook on Low for 6 hours.
2. Divide into bowls and serve for breakfast.

per serving: 292 calories, 2.4g protein, 32.4g carbohydrates, 19.5g fat, 5.8g fiber, 0mg cholesterol, 14mg sodium, 401mg potassium.

Spiced Bowls

Preparation time: 10 minutes
Cooking time: 4 hours
Servings: 2

Ingredients:

- ½ cup oatmeal
- ¼ cup coconut cream
- 2 tablespoons honey
- 2 tablespoons pumpkin puree
- 1 teaspoon ground cinnamon
- ½ teaspoon nutmeg, ground

Directions:

1. In your slow cooker, mix the oatmeal with the cream, honey, and the other ingredients, toss, put the lid on and cook on Low for 4 hours.
2. Divide into bowls and serve for breakfast.

per serving: 377 calories, 6.5g protein, 61g carbohydrates, 13.7g fat, 4.5g fiber, 13mg cholesterol, 251mg sodium, 171mg potassium.

Spices and Beef Mix

Preparation time: 10 minutes
Cooking time: 6 hours
Servings: 4

Ingredients:
- 1-pound beef sirloin, ground
- 4 eggs, whisked
- 1 tablespoon basil, chopped
- ½ teaspoon cumin powder
- 1 tablespoon chili powder
- 1 red onion, chopped
- 1 tablespoon olive oil

Directions:
1. Grease the slow cooker with the oil and mix the beef with the eggs, basil, and the other ingredients inside.
2. Toss, put the lid on, cook on Low for 6 hours, divide into bowls, and serve for breakfast.

per serving: 322 calories,40.5g protein, 4.1g carbohydrates, 15.4g fat, 1.3g fiber, 265mg cholesterol, 157mg sodium, 598mg potassium.

Cauliflower Casserole

Preparation time: 10 minutes
Cooking time: 5 hours
Servings: 2

Ingredients:
- 1-pound cauliflower florets
- 3 eggs, whisked
- 1 red onion, sliced
- ½ teaspoon sweet paprika
- ½ teaspoon turmeric powder
- 1 garlic clove, minced
- Cooking spray

Directions:
1. Spray your slow cooker with the cooking spray, and mix the cauliflower with the eggs, onion, and the other ingredients inside.
2. Put the lid on, cook on Low for 5 hours, divide between 2 plates, and serve for breakfast.

per serving: 179 calories,13.6g protein, 18.8g carbohydrates, 7g fat, 7.2g fiber, 246mg cholesterol, 163mg sodium, 888mg potassium.

Beef Meatloaf

Preparation time: 10 minutes
Cooking time: 4 hours
Servings: 4

Ingredients:

- 1 red onion, chopped
- 1-pound beef sirloin, minced
- ½ teaspoon chili powder
- 1 egg, whisked
- ½ teaspoon olive oil
- ½ teaspoon sweet paprika
- 2 tablespoons almond flour
- ½ teaspoon oregano, chopped
- ½ tablespoon basil, chopped
- ½ teaspoon marjoram, dried

Directions:

1. In a bowl, mix the beef with the onion, chili powder, and the other ingredients except for the oil, stir well and shape your meatloaf.
2. Grease a loaf pan that fits your slow cooker with the oil, add meatloaf mix into the pan, put it in your slow cooker, put the lid on, and cook on Low for 4 hours.
3. Slice and serve for breakfast.

per serving: 266 calories,37g protein, 3.9g carbohydrates, 10.6g fat, 1.3g fiber, 142mg cholesterol, 96mg sodium, 529mg potassium.

Quinoa and Chia Pudding

Preparation time: 10 minutes
Cooking time: 6 hours
Servings: 5

Ingredients:

- 1 cup coconut cream
- 2 tablespoons chia seeds
- ½ cup organic almond milk
- 1 tablespoon honey
- ½ cup quinoa, rinsed
- ½ teaspoon vanilla extract

Directions:

1. In your slow cooker, mix the cream with the chia seeds and the other ingredients, toss, put the lid on and cook on Low for 6 hours.
2. Divide into 2 bowls and serve for breakfast.

per serving: 221 calories,4.6g protein, 20.3g carbohydrates, 14.5g fat, 4.3g fiber, 0mg cholesterol, 24mg sodium, 266mg potassium.

Cilantro Casserole

Preparation time: 10 minutes
Cooking time: 4 hours
Servings: 2

Ingredients:
- 1 cup leek, chopped
- Cooking spray
- ½ cup mozzarella, shredded
- 1 garlic clove, minced
- 4 eggs, whisked
- 1 cup beef sausage, homemade, chopped
- 1 tablespoon cilantro, chopped

Directions:
1. Grease the slow cooker with the cooking spray and mix the leek with the mozzarella and the other ingredients inside.
2. Toss, spread into the pot, put the lid on, and cook on Low for 4 hours.
3. Divide between plates and serve for breakfast.

per serving: 197 calories,15.1g protein, 7.8g carbohydrates, 12g fat, 0.8g fiber, 337mg cholesterol, 224mg sodium, 226mg potassium.

Cherries and Honey Oats

Preparation time: 10 minutes
Cooking time: 7 hours
Servings: 2

Ingredients:
- 1 cup organic almond milk
- ½ cup oatmeal
- 1 tablespoon cocoa powder
- ½ cup cherries pitted
- 2 tablespoons honey
- ¼ teaspoon vanilla extract

Directions:
1. In your slow cooker, mix the organic almond milk with the cherries and the other ingredients, toss, put the lid on and cook on Low for 7 hours.
2. Divide into 2 bowls and serve for breakfast.

per serving: 438 calories,6.2g protein, 42.8g carbohydrates, 30.3g fat, 6.1g fiber, 0mg cholesterol, 23mg sodium, 468mg potassium.

Eggs and Chives Mix

Preparation time: 10 minutes
Cooking time: 6 hours
Servings: 2

Ingredients:

- ½ red onion, chopped
- ½ green bell pepper, chopped
- 2 sweet potatoes, peeled and grated
- ½ red bell pepper, chopped
- 1 garlic clove, minced
- ½ teaspoon olive oil
- 4 eggs, whisked
- 1 tablespoon chives, chopped
- A pinch of red pepper, crushed

Directions:

1. In a bowl, mix the eggs with the onion, bell peppers, and the other ingredients except for the oil and whisk well.
2. Grease your slow cooker with the oil, add the eggs and potato mix, spread, put the lid on, and cook on Low for 6 hours.
3. Divide everything between plates and serve.

per serving: 248 calories,13g protein, 27g carbohydrates, 10.2g fat, 4.1g fiber, 327mg cholesterol, 132mg sodium, 837mg potassium.

Sweet Coconut Spread

Preparation time: 10 minutes
Cooking time: 4 hours
Servings: 2

Ingredients:

- 2 apples, cored, peeled, and pureed
- ½ cup coconut cream
- 2 tablespoons apple cider
- 2 tablespoons honey
- ¼ teaspoon ground cinnamon
- ½ teaspoon lemon juice
- ¼ teaspoon ginger, grated

Directions:

1. In your slow cooker, mix the apple puree with the cream, honey, and the other ingredients, whisk, put the lid on and cook on High for 4 hours.
2. Blend using an immersion blender, cool down, and serve for breakfast.

per serving: 327 calories,2.1g protein, 53.7g carbohydrates, 14.7g fat, 7g fiber, 0mg cholesterol, 13mg sodium, 432mg potassium.

Spinach and Chili Powder Salad

Preparation time: 10 minutes
Cooking time: 6 hours
Servings: 4

Ingredients:

- 1 cup black beans, drained
- 1 cup red kidney beans, drained
- 1 cup baby spinach
- 2 spring onions, chopped
- ½ red bell pepper, chopped
- ¼ teaspoon turmeric powder
- ½ teaspoon garam masala
- ¼ cup vegetable stock
- A pinch of cumin, ground
- A pinch of chili powder
- ½ cup of salsa

Directions:

1. In your slow cooker, mix the beans with the spinach, onions, and the other ingredients, toss, put the lid on and cook on High for 6 hours.
2. Divide the mix into bowls and serve for breakfast.

per serving: 339 calories,21.9g protein, 62.6g carbohydrates, 1.3g fat, 15.5g fiber, 0mg cholesterol, 214mg sodium, 1535mg potassium.

Basil Mix

Preparation time: 10 minutes
Cooking time: 8 hours and 10 minutes
Servings: 2

Ingredients:

- 4 eggs, whisked
- 1 yellow onion, chopped
- 2 spring onions, chopped
- 1 cup chicken sausage, chopped, homemade
- 1 cup broccoli florets
- 2 teaspoons basil, dried
- A drizzle of olive oil

Directions:

1. Heat a pan with the oil over medium-high heat, add the yellow onion and the sausage, toss, cook for 10 minutes and transfer to the slow cooker.
2. Add the eggs and the other ingredients, toss, put the lid on, and cook on Low for 8 hours.
3. Divide between plates and serve for breakfast.

per serving: 320 calories,23.7g protein, 15.3g carbohydrates, 17.8g fat, 3.2g fiber, 327mg cholesterol, 463mg sodium, 386mg potassium.

Nut and Coconut Cream Butter

Preparation time: 10 minutes
Cooking time: 4 hours
Servings: 4

Ingredients:

- 1 cup cashews, soaked overnight, drained and blended
- ½ cup coconut cream
- ¼ teaspoon ground cinnamon
- 1 teaspoon lemon zest, grated
- 2 tablespoons honey
- A pinch of ginger, ground

Directions:

1. In your slow cooker, mix the cashews with the cream and the other ingredients, whisk, put the lid on and cook on High for 4 hours.
2. Blend using an immersion blender, divide into jars, and serve for breakfast cold.

per serving: 298 calories,6g protein, 21.7g carbohydrates, 23g fat, 1.8g fiber, 0mg cholesterol, 10mg sodium, 280mg potassium.

Pumpkin and Nutmeg Bowls

Preparation time: 10 minutes
Cooking time: 4 hours
Servings: 2

Ingredients:

- ½ cup coconut cream
- 1 ½ cups pumpkin, peeled and cubed
- 1 cup blackberries
- 2 tablespoons honey
- ¼ teaspoon nutmeg, ground
- ½ teaspoon vanilla extract

Directions:

3. In your slow cooker, combine the pumpkin with the berries, cream, and the other ingredients, toss, put the lid on and cook on Low for 4 hours.
4. Divide into bowls and serve for breakfast!

per serving: 300 calories,4.5g protein, 42.7g carbohydrates, 15.3g fat, 10.6g fiber, 0mg cholesterol, 20mg sodium, 666mg potassium.

Zucchini Mix

Preparation time: 10 minutes
Cooking time: 6 hours
Servings: 2

Ingredients:

- 2 spring onions, chopped
- 4 eggs, whisked
- ½ cup cauliflower florets
- 1 zucchini, grated
- ¼ cup tofu, crumbled
- ¼ cup coconut cream
- 1 tablespoon chives, chopped
- Cooking spray

Directions:

1. Grease the slow cooker with the cooking spray and mix the eggs with the spring onions, cauliflower, and the other ingredients inside.
2. Put the lid on and cook on Low for 6 hours.
3. Divide the mix between plates and serve for breakfast.

per serving: 244 calories,16.4g protein, 8.7g carbohydrates, 17.5g fat, 3.1g fiber, 327mg cholesterol, 151mg sodium, 622mg potassium.

Scallions Bowls

Preparation time: 10 minutes
Cooking time: 4 hours
Servings: 4

Ingredients:

- 1 cup quinoa
- 2 cups vegetable stock
- 4 scallions, chopped
- 2 carrots, peeled and grated
- 1 tablespoon olive oil
- 3 eggs, whisked
- 2 tablespoons tofu
- 2 tablespoons coconut cream

Directions:

1. In a bowl mix the eggs with the cream, tofu, and whisk.
2. Grease the slow cooker with the oil, add the quinoa, scallions, carrots, and the stock, stir, put the lid on and cook on Low for 2 hours.
3. Add the eggs mix, stir the whole thing, cook on Low for 2 more hours, divide into bowls, and serve for breakfast.

per serving: 277 calories,11.7g protein, 32.6g carbohydrates, 11.6g fat, 4.6g fiber, 123mg cholesterol, 99mg sodium, 454mg potassium.

Tofu Quiche

Preparation time: 10 minutes
Cooking time: 6 hours
Servings: 4

Ingredients:

- 2 cups baby Bella mushrooms, chopped
- ½ cup tofu, crumbled
- 4 eggs, whisked
- ½ cup coconut cream
- 1 tablespoon basil, chopped
- 2 tablespoons chives, chopped
- ½ cup almond flour
- ¼ teaspoons baking soda
- Cooking spray

Directions:

1. In a bowl, mix the eggs with the cream, flour, and the other ingredients except for the cooking spray and stir well.
2. Grease the slow cooker with the cooking spray, pour the quiche mix, spread well, put the lid on, and cook on High for 6 hours.
3. Slice the quiche, divide between plates and serve for breakfast.

per serving: 250 calories, 13g protein, 7.8g carbohydrates, 19.6g fat, 3.1g fiber, 164mg cholesterol, 157mg sodium, 399mg potassium.

Spiced Oatmeal with Pumpkin Puree

Preparation time: 10 minutes
Cooking time: 9 hours
Servings: 4

Ingredients:

- Cooking spray
- 1 cup steel-cut oats
- ½ cup organic almond milk
- 4 cups of water
- 2 tablespoons honey
- ½ cup pumpkin puree
- ½ teaspoon cinnamon powder
- A pinch of cloves, ground
- A pinch of ginger, grated
- A pinch of allspice, ground
- A pinch of nutmeg, ground

Directions:

1. Grease your Slow cooker with cooking spray, add oats, milk, water, honey, pumpkin puree, cinnamon, cloves, ginger, allspice, and nutmeg, cover, and cook on Low for 9 hours.
2. Stir your oatmeal, divide into bowls and serve for breakfast.

per serving: 99 calories, 2.1g protein, 20.1g carbohydrates, 1.6g fat, 2.2g fiber, 0mg cholesterol, 49mg sodium, 157mg potassium.

Salsa and Peppers Mix

Preparation time: 10 minutes
Cooking time: 3 hours
Servings: 4

Ingredients:

- ½ cup of brown rice
- 1 cup chicken stock
- 2 spring onions, chopped
- ½ orange bell pepper, chopped
- ½ red bell pepper, chopped
- ½ green bell pepper, chopped
- 2 ounces green chilies, chopped
- ½ cup canned black beans, drained
- ½ cup mild salsa
- ½ teaspoon sweet paprika
- ½ teaspoon lime zest, grated

Directions:

1. In your slow cooker, mix the rice with the stock, spring onions, and the other ingredients, toss, put the lid on and cook on High for 3 hours.
2. Divide the mix into bowls and serve for breakfast.

per serving: 241 calories, 9.7g protein, 48.3g carbohydrates, 2.2g fat, 9.8g fiber, 0mg cholesterol, 387mg sodium, 812mg potassium.

Breakfast Bowls

Preparation time: 10 minutes
Cooking time: 3 hours and 10 minutes
Servings: 8

Ingredients:

- 2 spring onions, chopped
- ½ green bell pepper, chopped
- ½ red bell pepper, chopped
- ½ yellow onion, chopped
- 5 ounces black beans, drained
- 5 ounces red kidney beans, drained
- 5 ounces pinto beans, drained
- ½ teaspoon turmeric powder
- 1 teaspoon chili powder
- 1 tablespoon olive oil

Directions:

1. Heat a pan with the oil over medium-high heat, add the spring onions, bell peppers, and the onion, sauté for 10 minutes and transfer to the slow cooker.
2. Add the beans and the other ingredients, toss, put the lid on and cook on High for 3 hours.
3. Divide the mix into bowls and serve for breakfast.

per serving: 205 calories,11.9g protein, 34.7g carbohydrates, 2.5g fat, 8.6g fiber, 0mg cholesterol, 10mg sodium, 795mg potassium.

Vegetable Recipes

Beets and Carrots Bowls

Preparation time: 10 minutes
Cooking time: 7 hours
Servings: 8

Ingredients:

- 2 tablespoons stevia
- ¾ cup pomegranate juice
- 2 teaspoons ginger, grated
- 2 and ½ pounds beets, peeled and cut into wedges
- 12 ounces' carrots, cut into medium wedges

Directions:

1. In your Slow cooker, mix beets with carrots, ginger, stevia, and pomegranate juice, toss, cover, and cook on Low for 7 hours.
2. Divide between plates and serve as a side dish.

per serving: 95 calories,2.8g protein, 22.1g carbohydrates, 0.3g fat, 4g fiber, 0mg cholesterol, 140mg sodium, 631mg potassium.

Italian Style Vegetable Mix

Preparation time: 10 minutes
Cooking time: 6 hours
Servings: 8

Ingredients:

- 38 ounces canned cannellini beans, drained
- 1 yellow onion, chopped
- ¼ cup basil pesto
- 19 oz fava beans, cooked
- 4 garlic cloves, minced
- 1 ½ teaspoon Italian seasoning, dried and crushed
- 1 tomato, chopped
- 2 cups spinach
- 1 cup radicchio, torn

Directions:

1. In your Slow cooker, mix cannellini beans with fava beans, basil pesto, onion, garlic, Italian seasoning, tomato, spinach, and radicchio, toss, cover, and cook on Low for 6 hours.
2. Divide between plates and serve as a side dish.

per serving: 690 calories,50g protein, 122.7g carbohydrates, 2.2g fat, 51g fiber, 0mg cholesterol, 49mg sodium, 2712mg potassium.

Wild Rice Pilaf

Preparation time: 10 minutes
Cooking time: 7 hours
Servings: 12

Ingredients:

- ½ cup wild rice
- ½ cup barley
- 2/3 cup wheat berries
- 27 ounces vegetable stock
- 2 cups baby lima beans
- 1 red bell pepper, chopped
- 1 yellow onion, chopped
- 1 tablespoon olive oil
- 1 teaspoon sage, dried and crushed
- 4 garlic cloves, minced

Directions:

1. In your Slow cooker, mix rice with barley, wheat berries, lima beans, bell pepper, onion, oil, sage, and garlic, stir, cover, and cook on Low for 7 hours.
2. Stir one more time, divide between plates and serve as a side dish.

per serving: 115 calories,4.7g protein, 21g carbohydrates, 1.8g fat, 3.8g fiber, 0mg cholesterol, 37mg sodium, 231mg potassium.

Apples Mix

Preparation time: 10 minutes
Cooking time: 7 hours
Servings: 10

Ingredients:

- 2 green apples, cored and cut into wedges
- 3 pounds sweet potatoes, peeled and cut into medium wedges
- 1 cup coconut cream
- 1 cup apple butter
- 1 and ½ teaspoon pumpkin pie spice

Directions:

1. In your Slow cooker, mix sweet potatoes with green apples, cream, apple butter, and spice, toss, cover, and cook on Low for 7 hours.
2. Toss, divide between plates, and serve as a side dish.

per serving: 288 calories,2.9g protein, 57.4g carbohydrates, 6.1g fat, 7.6g fiber, 0mg cholesterol, 20mg sodium, 1247mg potassium.

Asparagus Mix

Preparation time: 10 minutes
Cooking time: 5 hours
Servings: 4

Ingredients:
- 2-pound asparagus spears, cut into medium pieces
- 1 cup mushrooms, sliced
- A drizzle of olive oil
- 2 cups of coconut milk
- 5 eggs, whisked

Directions:
1. Grease your Slow cooker with the oil and spread asparagus and mushrooms on the bottom.
2. In a bowl, mix the eggs with milk, and whisk, pour into the slow cooker, toss everything, cover and cook on Low for 6 hours.
3. Divide between plates and serve as a side dish.

per serving: 404 calories, 15.2g protein, 65.5g carbohydrates, 34.4g fat, 7.6g fiber, 205mg cholesterol, 101mg sodium, 903mg potassium.

Asparagus and Eggs Mix

Preparation time: 10 minutes
Cooking time: 6 hours
Servings: 4

Ingredients:
- 10 ounces cream of celery
- 12 ounces asparagus, chopped
- 2 eggs, hard-boiled, peeled, and sliced
- 5 oz tofu, crumbled
- 1 teaspoon olive oil

Directions:
1. Grease your Slow cooker with the oil, add cream of celery and tofu to the slow cooker and stir.
2. Add asparagus and eggs, cover, and cook on Low for 6 hours.
3. Divide between plates and serve as a side dish.

per serving: 134 calories, 8.5g protein, 9.1g carbohydrates, 8.1g fat, 2.5g fiber, 90mg cholesterol, 573mg sodium, 323mg potassium.

Classic Vegetable Meals

Preparation time: 10 minutes
Cooking time: 3 hours
Servings: 4

Ingredients:

- 1 and ½ cups red onion, cut into medium chunks
- 1 cup cherry tomatoes, halved
- 2 and ½ cups zucchini, sliced
- 2 cups yellow bell pepper, chopped
- 1 cup mushrooms, sliced
- 2 tablespoons basil, chopped
- 1 tablespoon thyme, chopped
- ½ cup olive oil
- ½ cup balsamic vinegar

Directions:

1. In your Slow cooker, mix onion pieces with tomatoes, zucchini, bell pepper, mushrooms, basil, thyme, oil, and vinegar, toss to coat everything, cover, and cook on High for 3 hours.
2. Divide between plates and serve as a side dish.

per serving: 295 calories, 3.8g protein, 16.3g carbohydrates, 25.8g fat, 4.3g fiber, 0mg cholesterol, 22mg sodium, 739mg potassium.

Okra and Tomato Sauce Mix

Preparation time: 10 minutes
Cooking time: 8 hours
Servings: 4

Ingredients:

- 2 garlic cloves, minced
- 1 yellow onion, chopped
- 14 ounces tomato sauce
- 1 teaspoon sweet paprika
- 2 cups okra, sliced

Directions:

1. In your Slow cooker, mix garlic with the onion, tomato sauce, paprika, okra, cover, and cook on Low for 8 hours.
2. Divide between plates and serve as a side dish.

per serving: 59 calories, 2.8g protein, 12.4g carbohydrates, 0.4g fat, 3.9g fiber, 0mg cholesterol, 525mg sodium, 537mg potassium.

Stewed Okra with Cayenne Pepper

Preparation time: 10 minutes
Cooking time: 3 hours
Servings: 4

Ingredients:
- 2 cups okra, sliced
- 2 garlic cloves, minced
- 6 ounces tomato sauce
- 1 red onion, chopped
- A pinch of cayenne peppers

Directions:
1. In your Slow cooker, mix okra with garlic, onion, cayenne, tomato sauce, cover, cook on Low for 3 hours.
2. Divide between plates and serve as a side dish.

per serving: 43 calories,1.9g protein, 9.1g carbohydrates, 0.2g fat, 2.9g fiber, 0mg cholesterol, 228mg sodium, 336mg potassium.

Okra and Mushrooms Side Dish

Preparation time: 10 minutes
Cooking time: 3 hours
Servings: 4

Ingredients:
- 2 cups okra, sliced
- 1 and ½ cups red onion, roughly chopped
- 1 cup cherry tomatoes, halved
- 2 ½ cups zucchini, sliced
- 2 cups bell peppers, sliced
- 1 cup white mushrooms, sliced
- ½ cup olive oil
- ½ cup balsamic vinegar
- 2 tablespoons basil, chopped
- 1 tablespoon thyme, chopped

Directions:
1. In your Slow cooker, mix okra with onion, tomatoes, zucchini, bell peppers, mushrooms, basil, and thyme.
2. In a bowl mix oil with vinegar, whisk well, add to the slow cooker, cover and cook on High for 3 hours.
3. Divide between plates and serve as a side dish.

per serving: 304 calories,3.9g protein, 17.7g carbohydrates, 25.8g fat, 5.1g fiber, 0mg cholesterol, 19mg sodium, 703mg potassium.

Okra and Corn Bowls

Preparation time: 10 minutes
Cooking time: 8 hours
Servings: 4

Ingredients:

- 3 garlic cloves, minced
- 1 small green bell pepper, chopped
- 1 small yellow onion, chopped
- 1 cup of water
- 16 ounces okra, sliced
- 2 cups corn kernels
- 1 and ½ teaspoon smoked paprika
- 28 ounces canned tomatoes, crushed
- 1 teaspoon oregano, dried
- 1 teaspoon thyme, dried
- 1 teaspoon marjoram, dried
- A pinch of cayenne pepper

Directions:

1. In your Slow cooker, mix garlic with bell pepper, onion, water, okra, corn, paprika, tomatoes, oregano, thyme, marjoram, and pepper, cover, cook on Low for 8 hours, divide between plates and serve as a side dish.

per serving: 171 calories,7.3g protein, 36.2g carbohydrates, 1.8g fat, 9.6g fiber, 0mg cholesterol, 33mg sodium, 1138mg potassium.

Roasted Beets with Olive Oil

Preparation time: 10 minutes
Cooking time: 4 hours
Servings: 5

Ingredients:

- 10 small beets
- 5 teaspoons olive oil

Directions:

1. Divide each beet on a tin foil piece, drizzle oil, wrap beets in the foil, place them in your Slow cooker, cover and cook on High for 4 hours.
2. Unwrap beets, cool them down a bit, peel, slice and serve them as a side dish.

per serving: 128 calories,3.4g protein, 19.9g carbohydrates, 5g fat, 4g fiber, 0mg cholesterol, 154mg sodium, 610mg potassium.

Thyme Beets with Garlic

Preparation time: 10 minutes
Cooking time: 6 hours
Servings: 8

Ingredients:

- 12 small beets, peeled and sliced
- ¼ cup of water
- 4 garlic cloves, minced
- 2 tablespoons olive oil
- 1 teaspoon thyme, dried
- 1 tablespoon fresh thyme, chopped

Directions:

1. In your Slow cooker, mix beets with water, garlic, oil, dried thyme, cover, and cook on Low for 6 hours.
2. Divide beets on plates, sprinkle fresh thyme all over, and serve as a side dish.

per serving: 99 calories,2.6g protein, 15.5g carbohydrates, 3.8g fat, 3.1g fiber, 0mg cholesterol, 116mg sodium, 465mg potassium.

Beets and Honey Side Salad

Preparation time: 10 minutes
Cooking time: 7 hours
Servings: 12

Ingredients:

- 5 beets, peeled and sliced
- ¼ cup balsamic vinegar
- 1/3 cup honey
- 1 tablespoon rosemary, chopped
- 2 tablespoons olive oil
- 2 garlic cloves, minced

Directions:

1. In your Slow cooker, mix beets with vinegar, honey, oil, rosemary, and garlic, cover, and cook on Low for 7 hours.
2. Divide between plates and serve as a side dish.

per serving: 70 calories,0.8g protein, 12.3g carbohydrates, 2.5g fat, 1g fiber, 0mg cholesterol, 33mg sodium, 140mg potassium.

Lemony Beets with White Vinegar

Preparation time: 10 minutes
Cooking time: 8 hours
Servings: 6

Ingredients:
- 6 beets, peeled and cut into medium wedges
- 2 tablespoons honey
- 2 tablespoons olive oil
- 2 tablespoons lemon juice
- 1 tablespoon white vinegar
- ½ teaspoon lemon peel, grated

Directions:
1. In your Slow cooker, mix beets with honey, oil, lemon juice, vinegar, and lemon peel, cover, and cook on Low for 8 hours.
2. Divide between plates and serve as a side dish.

per serving: 107 calories,1.7g protein, 15.9g carbohydrates, 4.9g fat, 2g fiber, 0mg cholesterol, 78mg sodium, 317mg potassium.

Carrot Side Salad

Preparation time: 10 minutes
Cooking time: 7 hours
Servings: 6

Ingredients:
- ½ cup walnuts, chopped
- ¼ cup lemon juice
- ½ cup olive oil
- 1 shallot, chopped
- 1 teaspoon Dijon mustard
- 1 tablespoon honey
- 2 beets, peeled and cut into wedges
- 2 carrots, peeled and sliced
- 1 cup parsley
- 5 ounces arugula

Directions:
1. In your Slow cooker, mix beets with carrots, honey, mustard, shallot, oil, lemon juice, and walnuts, cover, and cook on Low for 7 hours.
2. Transfer everything to a bowl, add parsley and arugula, toss, divide between plates and serve as a side dish.

per serving: 256 calories,4.3g protein, 11.3g carbohydrates, 23.4g fat, 2.7g fiber, 0mg cholesterol, 64mg sodium, 385mg potassium.

Cauliflower Gratin

Preparation time: 10 minutes
Cooking time: 7 hours
Servings: 12

Ingredients:
- 16 ounces baby carrots
- 6 tablespoons pumpkin puree
- 1 cauliflower head, florets separated
- 1 yellow onion, chopped
- 1 teaspoon mustard powder
- 1 ½ cups coconut milk
- 6 ounces tofu, crumbled

Directions:
1. Put the pumpkin puree in your Slow cooker, add carrots, cauliflower, onion, mustard powder, and coconut milk, and toss.
2. Sprinkle tofu all over, cover, and cook on Low for 7 hours.
3. Divide between plates and serve as a side dish.

per serving: 105 calories,2.8g protein, 7.8g carbohydrates, 7.9g fat, 2.9g fiber, 0mg cholesterol, 43mg sodium, 287mg potassium.

Tarragon Beets

Preparation time: 10 minutes
Cooking time: 7 hours
Servings: 4

Ingredients:
- 6 medium assorted-color beets, peeled and cut into wedges
- 2 tablespoons balsamic vinegar
- 2 tablespoons olive oil
- 2 tablespoons chives, chopped
- 1 tablespoon tarragon, chopped
- 1 teaspoon orange peel, grated

Directions:
1. In your Slow cooker, mix beets with vinegar, oil, chives, tarragon, and orange peel, cover, and cook on Low for 7 hours.
2. Divide between plates and serve as a side dish.

per serving: 130 calories,2.7g protein, 15.4g carbohydrates, 7.3g fat, 3.1g fiber, 0mg cholesterol, 116mg sodium, 482mg potassium.

Summer Mix

Preparation time: 10 minutes
Cooking time: 2 hours
Servings: 4

Ingredients:

- ¼ cup olive oil
- 2 tablespoons basil, chopped
- 2 tablespoons balsamic vinegar
- 2 garlic cloves, minced
- 2 teaspoons mustard
- 3 summer squash, sliced
- 2 zucchinis, sliced

Directions:

1. In your Slow cooker, mix squash with zucchinis, mustard, garlic, vinegar, basil, and oil, toss a bit, cover, and cook on High for 2 hours.
2. Divide between plates and serve as a side dish.

per serving: 154 calories, 2.7g protein, 8.2g carbohydrates, 13.5g fat, 2.4g fiber, 0mg cholesterol, 13mg sodium, 495mg potassium.

Squash Side Salad

Preparation time: 10 minutes
Cooking time: 2 hours
Servings: 4

Ingredients:

- 2 garlic cloves, minced
- ½ cup olive oil
- ¼ cup basil, chopped
- 1 red bell pepper, chopped
- 1 eggplant, roughly chopped
- 1 summer squash, cubed
- 1 Vidalia onion, cut into wedges
- 1 zucchini, sliced
- 1 green bell pepper, chopped

Directions:

1. In your Slow cooker, mix red bell pepper with green one, squash, zucchini, eggplant, onion, basil, oil, and garlic, toss gently, cover, and cook on High for 2 hours.
2. Divide between plates and serve as a side dish.

per serving: 282 calories, 2.8g protein, 15g carbohydrates, 25.7g fat, 6g fiber, 0mg cholesterol, 10mg sodium, 568mg potassium.

Italian Squash Mix

Preparation time: 10 minutes
Cooking time: 1 hour and 30 minutes
Servings: 4

Ingredients:

- 12 small squash, peeled and cut into wedges
- 2 red bell peppers, cut into wedges
- 2 green bell peppers, cut into wedges
- 1/3 cup Italian dressing
- 1 red onion, cut into wedges
- 1 tablespoon parsley, chopped

Directions:

1. In your Slow cooker, mix squash with red bell peppers, green bell peppers, and Italian dressing, cover, and cook on High for 1 hour and 30 minutes.
2. Add parsley, toss, divide between plates and serve as a side dish.

per serving: 144 calories, 5.3g protein, 21g carbohydrates, 6.4g fat, 5.3g fiber, 13mg cholesterol, 44mg sodium, 1094mg potassium.

Green Beans Bowls

Preparation time: 10 minutes
Cooking time: 2 hours
Servings: 2

Ingredients:

- 2 cups green beans, halved
- 1 red bell pepper, cut into strips
- 1 tablespoon olive oil
- 1 and ½ tablespoon honey mustard

Directions:

1. In your Slow cooker, mix green beans with bell pepper, oil, and honey mustard, toss, cover, and cook on High for 2 hours.
2. Divide between plates and serve as a side dish.

per serving: 136 calories, 2.6g protein, 16.8g carbohydrates, 7.3g fat, 4.5g fiber, 0mg cholesterol, 64mg sodium, 342mg potassium.

Garlic Green Beans

Preparation time: 10 minutes
Cooking time: 2 hours
Servings: 6

Ingredients:
- 22 ounces green beans
- 2 garlic cloves, minced
- ¼ cup peanut butter
- 2 tablespoons parmesan, grated

Directions:
1. In your Slow cooker, mix green beans with garlic, pumpkin puree, and parmesan, toss, cover, and cook on High for 2 hours.
2. Divide between plates, sprinkle parmesan all over, and serve as a side dish.

per serving: 112 calories,6.1g protein, 10g carbohydrates, 6.5g fat, 4.2g fiber, 3mg cholesterol, 99mg sodium, 291mg potassium.

Zucchini and Yogurt Casserole

Preparation time: 10 minutes
Cooking time: 2 hours
Servings: 10

Ingredients:
- 7 cups zucchini, sliced
- 2 tablespoons pumpkin puree
- 1/3 cup yellow onion, chopped
- 6 oz tofu, crumbled
- 1 cup chicken stock
- 1/3 cup Greek-style yogurt
- 1 tablespoon parsley, chopped
- Cooking spray

Directions:
1. Grease your Slow cooker with cooking spray and arrange zucchini and onion in the pot.
2. Add pumpkin puree, stock, Greek-style yogurt, and toss.
3. Cook on High for 2 hours.
4. Divide zucchini casserole on plates, sprinkle parsley all over, and serve as a side dish.

per serving: 28 calories,2.5g protein, 3.9g carbohydrates, 0.9g fat, 1.2g fiber, 1mg cholesterol, 90mg sodium, 260mg potassium.

Nut Salad

Preparation time: 10 minutes
Cooking time: 1 hour
Servings: 4

Ingredients:

- 2 cups strawberries, halved
- 2 tablespoons mint, chopped
- 1/3 cup raspberry vinegar
- 2 tablespoons honey
- 1 tablespoon canola oil
- 4 cups spinach, torn
- ½ cup blueberries
- ¼ cup walnuts, chopped
- 1-ounce goat cheese, crumbled

Directions:

1. In your Slow cooker, mix strawberries with mint, vinegar, honey, oil, spinach, blueberries, and walnuts, cover, and cook on High for 1 hour.
2. Divide salad on plates, sprinkle cheese on top, and serve as a side dish.

per serving: 189 calories,5.6g protein, 19.3g carbohydrates, 11.1g fat, 3.3g fiber, 7mg cholesterol, 52mg sodium, 369mg potassium.

Blueberry Salad

Preparation time: 10 minutes
Cooking time: 1 hour
Servings: 3

Ingredients:

- ¼ cup pecans, chopped
- ½ teaspoon honey
- 2 teaspoons maple syrup
- 1 tablespoon white vinegar
- 2 tablespoons orange juice
- 1 tablespoon olive oil
- 4 cups spinach
- 2 oranges, peeled and cut into segments
- 1 cup blueberries

Directions:

1. In your Slow cooker, mix pecans with honey, maple syrup, vinegar, orange juice, oil, spinach, oranges, and blueberries, toss, cover, and cook on High for 1 hour.
2. Divide between plates and serve as a side dish.

per serving: 253 calories,4.2g protein, 29.9g carbohydrates, 15.2g fat, 6.5g fiber, 0mg cholesterol, 33mg sodium, 574mg potassium.

Farro Pilaf

Preparation time: 10 minutes
Cooking time: 5 hours
Servings: 12

Ingredients:
- 1 shallot, chopped
- 1 teaspoon garlic, minced
- A drizzle of olive oil
- 1 ½ cups whole grain farro
- ¾ cup wild rice
- 6 cups chicken stock
- 1 tablespoon parsley and sage, chopped
- ½ cup hazelnuts, toasted and chopped

Directions:
1. In your Slow cooker, mix oil with garlic, shallot, farro, rice, stock, sage and parsley, hazelnuts, and toss, cover, and cook on Low for 5 hours.
2. Divide between plates and serve as a side dish.

per serving: 131 calories,4.3g protein, 22.6g carbohydrates, 3.2g fat, 2.2g fiber, 0mg cholesterol, 385mg sodium, 75mg potassium.

Classic Pink Rice

Preparation time: 10 minutes
Cooking time: 5 hours
Servings: 8

Ingredients:
- 1 teaspoon salt
- 2 ½ cups of water
- 2 cups pink rice

Directions:
1. Put the rice in your Slow cooker add water and salt, stir, cover, and cook on Low for 5 hours
2. Stir rice a bit, divide it between plates and serve as a side dish.

per serving: 152 calories,3.1g protein, 33.3g carbohydrates, 1.2g fat, 1.5g fiber, 0mg cholesterol, 293mg sodium, 73mg potassium.

Pumpkin Rice with Nutmeg

Preparation time: 10 minutes
Cooking time: 5 hours
Servings: 6

Ingredients:
- 2 ounces olive oil
- 1 small yellow onion, chopped
- 2 garlic cloves, minced
- 12 ounces of brown rice
- 4 cups chicken stock
- 6 ounces pumpkin puree
- ½ teaspoon nutmeg, ground
- 1 teaspoon thyme, chopped
- ½ teaspoon ginger, grated
- ½ teaspoon ground cinnamon
- ½ teaspoon allspice, ground
- 4 ounces Greek-style yogurt

Directions:
1. In your Slow cooker, mix oil with onion, garlic, rice, stock, pumpkin puree, nutmeg, thyme, ginger, cinnamon, and allspice, stir, cover, and cook on Low for 4 hours and 30 minutes.
2. Add yogurt, stir, cover, cook on Low for 30 minutes more, divide between plates and serve as a side dish.

per serving: 318 calories, 7.3g protein, 48.7g carbohydrates, 10.9g fat, 3.3g fiber, 1mg cholesterol, 521mg sodium, 277mg potassium

Orange Rinds Carrots

Preparation time: 10 minutes
Cooking time: 6 hours
Servings: 2

Ingredients:
- ½ pound carrots, sliced
- ½ tablespoon olive oil
- ½ cup of orange juice
- ½ teaspoon orange rind, grated

Directions:
1. In your slow cooker, mix the carrots with the oil and the other ingredients, toss, put the lid on, and cook on Low for 6 hours.
2. Divide between plates and serve as a side dish.

per serving: 105 calories, 1.4g protein, 17.7g carbohydrates, 3.6g fat, 3g fiber, 0mg cholesterol, 79mg sodium, 488mg potassium.

Rice and Artichokes Mix

Preparation time: 10 minutes
Cooking time: 4 hours
Servings: 4

Ingredients:

- 1 tablespoon olive oil
- 5 ounces brown rice
- 2 garlic cloves, minced
- 1 ¼ cups chicken stock
- 1 ¼ cups of water
- 15 ounces artichoke hearts, chopped
- 16 ounces tofu, crumbled
- 1 tablespoon parmesan, grated
- 1 and ½ tablespoons thyme, chopped

Directions:

1. In your Slow cooker, mix oil with rice, garlic, stock, water, artichokes, and stir, cover, and cook on Low for 4 hours.
2. Add tofu, parmesan, and thyme, toss, divide between plates and serve as a side dish.

per serving: 315 calories,18g protein, 41.1g carbohydrates, 11g fat, 8g fiber, 5mg cholesterol, 421mg sodium, 668mg potassium.

Aromatic Saffron Risotto

Preparation time: 10 minutes
Cooking time: 2 hours
Servings: 2

Ingredients:

- ½ tablespoon olive oil
- ¼ teaspoon saffron powder
- 1 cup of brown rice
- 2 cups vegetable stock
- A pinch of ground cinnamon
- 1 tablespoon almonds, chopped

Directions:

1. In your slow cooker, mix the rice with the stock and the other ingredients, toss, put the lid on and cook on High for 2 hours.
2. Divide between plates and serve as a side dish.

per serving: 397 calories,8.2g protein, 73.9g carbohydrates, 7.6g fat, 4.1g fiber, 0mg cholesterol, 54mg sodium, 276mg potassium.

Green Beans Bowls

Preparation time: 10 minutes
Cooking time: 3 hours
Servings: 4

Ingredients:

- 1 pound fresh green beans, trimmed
- 1 small yellow onion, chopped
- 1 garlic clove, minced
- 1 cup chicken stock
- 8 ounces mushrooms, sliced
- A splash of balsamic vinegar

Directions:

1. In your Slow cooker, mix beans with onion, garlic, stock, mushrooms, and vinegar, stir, cover, and cook on Low for 3 hours.
2. Divide between plates and serve as a side dish.

per serving: 58 calories,4.3g protein, 12g carbohydrates, 0.5g fat, 4.8g fiber, 0mg cholesterol, 202mg sodium, 450mg potassium.

Green Onions and Farro

Preparation time: 10 minutes
Cooking time: 5 hours
Servings: 6

Ingredients:

- 1 tablespoon apple cider vinegar
- 1 cup whole-grain farro
- 1 teaspoon lemon juice
- 3 cups of water
- 1 tablespoon olive oil
- ¼ cup green onions, chopped
- 10 mint leaves, chopped
- 2 cups cherries, pitted and halved

Directions:

1. Put the water in your Slow cooker, add farro, stir, cover, cook on Low for 5 hours, drain and transfer to a bowl.
2. Add, oil, lemon juice, vinegar, fresh cherries, green onions, and mint, toss, divide between plates and serve as a side dish.

per serving: 124 calories,3.4g protein, 20.6g carbohydrates, 3.7g fat, 3.1g fiber, 0mg cholesterol, 14mg sodium, 103mg potassium.

Black Beans Bowls

Preparation time: 10 minutes
Cooking time: 7 hours
Servings: 8

Ingredients:
- 1 cup black beans, soaked overnight, drained, and rinsed
- 1 cup of water
- 1 spring onion, chopped
- 2 garlic cloves, minced
- ½ teaspoon cumin seeds

Directions:
1. In your Slow cooker, mix beans with water, onion, garlic, and cumin seeds, stir, cover, and cook on Low for 7 hours.
2. Divide everything between plates and serve as a side dish.

per serving: 85 calories,5.3g protein, 15.6g carbohydrates, 0.4g fat, 3.8g fiber, 0mg cholesterol, 3mg sodium, 370mg potassium.

Mexican Rice with Hot Pepper

Preparation time: 10 minutes
Cooking time: 4 hours
Servings: 8

Ingredients:
- 1 cup of brown rice
- 1 and ¼ cups vegetable stock
- ½ cup cilantro, chopped
- ½ avocado, pitted, peeled, and chopped
- ¼ cup hot red pepper sauce

Directions:
1. Put the rice in your Slow cooker, add the stock, stir, cover, cook on Low for 4 hours, fluff with a fork, and transfer to a bowl.
2. In your food processor, mix avocado with hot sauce and cilantro, blend well, pour over rice, toss well, divide between plates, and serve as a side dish.

per serving: 120 calories,2.1g protein, 20.9g carbohydrates, 3.1g fat, 1.8g fiber, 0mg cholesterol, 62mg sodium, 130mg potassium.

Rice and Beans Bowls

Preparation time: 20 minutes
Cooking time: 5 hours
Servings: 7

Ingredients:

- 1 pound red kidney beans, soaked overnight and drained
- 1 teaspoon olive oil
- 1 pound chicken sausage, roughly chopped
- 1 yellow onion, chopped
- 1 celery stalk, chopped
- 4 garlic cloves, chopped
- 1 green bell pepper, chopped
- 1 teaspoon thyme, dried
- 2 bay leaves
- 5 cups of water
- ½ cup brown rice, cooked
- 2 green onions, minced
- 2 tablespoons parsley, minced
- Hot sauce for serving

Directions:

1. In your Slow cooker, mix red beans with oil, sausage, onion, celery, garlic, bell pepper, thyme, bay leaves, and water, cover, and cook on Low for 5 hours.
2. Divide the rice between plates, add beans, sausage, and veggies on top, sprinkle green onions and parsley, and serve as a side dish with hot sauce drizzled all over.

per serving: 412 calories,24.6g protein, 58.3g carbohydrates, 8.9g fat, 11.6g fiber, 0mg cholesterol, 277mg sodium, 1006mg potassium.

Sweet Fruits Rice

Preparation time: 10 minutes
Cooking time: 2 hours
Servings: 2

Ingredients:

- 1 cup of brown rice
- 2 cups chicken stock
- ½ cup mango, chopped
- 1 teaspoon olive oil

Directions:

1. In your slow cooker, mix the rice with the stock and the other ingredients, toss, put the lid on and cook on High for 2 hours.
2. Divide between plates and serve as a side dish.

per serving: 398 calories,8.2g protein, 79.3g carbohydrates, 5.6g fat, 3.9g fiber, 0mg cholesterol, 768mg sodium, 338mg potassium.

Tender Farro Pilaf

Preparation time: 10 minutes
Cooking time: 4 hours
Servings: 2

Ingredients:
- ½ tablespoon balsamic vinegar
- ½ cup whole grain farro
- 1 cup chicken stock, low-sodium
- ½ tablespoon olive oil
- 1 tablespoon green onions, chopped
- 1 tablespoon mint, chopped

Directions:
1. In your slow cooker, mix the farro with the vinegar and the other ingredients, toss, put the lid on and cook on Low for 4 hours.
2. Divide between plates and serve.

per serving: 175 calories, 4.5g protein, 28.8g carbohydrates, 5.6g fat, 2.8g fiber, 0mg cholesterol, 388mg sodium, 31mg potassium.

Peanut Butter Quinoa Pilaf

Preparation time: 10 minutes
Cooking time: 2 hours
Servings: 2

Ingredients:
- 1 cup quinoa
- 2 teaspoons peanut butter
- 1 teaspoon turmeric powder
- 2 cups chicken stock
- 1 teaspoon cumin, ground

Directions:
1. Grease your slow cooker with the peanut butter, add the quinoa and the other ingredients, toss, put the lid on and cook on High for 2 hours.
2. Divide between plates and serve as a side dish.

per serving: 362 calories, 14.3g protein, 57.5g carbohydrates, 8.7g fat, 6.6g fiber, 0mg cholesterol, 795mg sodium, 574mg potassium.

Greens with Rice

Preparation time: 10 minutes
Cooking time: 2 hours
Servings: 4

Ingredients:
- 2 scallions, chopped
- 1 tablespoon olive oil
- 1 cup of brown rice
- 1 cup chicken stock
- 6 ounces spinach, chopped
- 2 ounces goat cheese, crumbled

Directions:
1. In your slow cooker, mix the rice with the stock and the other ingredients, toss, put the lid on and cook on High for 2 hours.
2. Divide between plates and serve as a side dish.

per serving: 281 calories, 9.4g protein, 38.8g carbohydrates, 10.1g fat, 2.8g fiber, 15mg cholesterol, 277mg sodium, 396mg potassium.

Creamy Parmesan Rice

Preparation time: 10 minutes
Cooking time: 2 hours and 30 minutes
Servings: 2

Ingredients:
- 1 cup of brown rice
- 2 cups chicken stock
- 1 tablespoon olive oil
- 1 red onion, chopped
- 1 tablespoon lemon juice
- 1 tablespoon parmesan, grated

Directions:
1. In your slow cooker, mix the rice with the stock, oil, and the other ingredients, toss, put the lid on and cook on High for 2 hours and 30 minutes.
2. Divide between plates and serve as a side dish.

per serving: 482 calories, 13g protein, 78.9g carbohydrates, 13.g fat, 4.4g fiber, 10mg cholesterol, 901mg sodium, 359mg potassium.

Lemon Zest Artichokes

Preparation time: 10 minutes
Cooking time: 3 hours
Servings: 2

Ingredients:
- 1 cup vegetable stock, low-sodium
- 2 medium artichokes, trimmed
- 1 tablespoon lemon juice
- 1 tablespoon lemon zest, grated

Directions:
1. In your slow cooker, mix the artichokes with the stock and the other ingredients, toss, put the lid on and cook on Low for 3 hours.
2. Divide artichokes between plates and serve as a side dish.

per serving: 90 calories,5.9g protein, 19.8g carbohydrates, 0.3g fat, 9.5g fiber, 0mg cholesterol, 223mg sodium, 682mg potassium.

Chili Bok Choy

Preparation time: 10 minutes
Cooking time: 1 hour
Servings: 2

Ingredients:
- 1 pound bok choy, torn
- ½ cup chicken stock
- ½ teaspoon chili powder
- 1 garlic clove, minced
- 1 teaspoon ginger, grated
- 1 tablespoon coconut oil

Directions:
1. In your slow cooker, mix the bok choy with the stock and the other ingredients, toss, put the lid on and cook on High for 1 hour.
2. Divide between plates and serve as a side dish.

per serving: 98 calories,3.8g protein, 6.6g carbohydrates, 7.6g fat, 2.6g fiber, 0mg cholesterol, 345mg sodium, 606mg potassium.

Yogurt Eggplant

Preparation time: 10 minutes
Cooking time: 2 hours
Servings: 2

Ingredients:
- 2 small eggplants, roughly cubed
- ½ cup Greek-style yogurt
- 1 tablespoon olive oil
- A pinch of hot pepper flakes
- 2 tablespoons oregano, chopped

Directions:
1. In your slow cooker, mix the eggplants with the yogurt and the other ingredients, toss, put the lid on and cook on High for 2 hours.
2. Divide between plates and serve as a side dish.

per serving: 281 calories, 8.1g protein, 38.9g carbohydrates, 13.4g fat, 21.3g fiber, 20mg cholesterol, 37mg sodium, 1424mg potassium.

Cabbage Mix

Preparation time: 10 minutes
Cooking time: 2 hours
Servings: 2

Ingredients:
- 1 ½ cups green cabbage, shredded
- 1 cup red cabbage, shredded
- 1 tablespoon olive oil
- 1 red onion, sliced
- 2 spring onions, chopped
- ½ cup tomato paste
- ¼ cup vegetable stock
- 2 tomatoes, chopped
- 2 jalapenos, chopped
- 1 tablespoon chili powder
- 1 tablespoon chives, chopped

Directions:
1. Grease your slow cooker with the oil and mix the cabbage with the onion, spring onions, and the other ingredients inside.
2. Toss, put the lid on, and cook on High for 2 hours.
3. Divide between plates and serve as a side dish.

per serving: 202 calories, 6.7g protein, 31.4g carbohydrates, 8.4g fat, 9.3g fiber, 0mg cholesterol, 192mg sodium, 1338mg potassium.

Basil and Thyme Okra Mix

Preparation time: 10 minutes
Cooking time: 2 hours
Servings: 4

Ingredients:
- 2 cups okra, sliced
- 1 cup cherry tomatoes, halved
- 1 tablespoon olive oil
- ½ teaspoon turmeric powder
- 2 tablespoons balsamic vinegar
- 2 tablespoons basil, chopped
- 1 tablespoon thyme, chopped

Directions:
1. In your slow cooker, mix the okra with the tomatoes, and the other ingredients, toss, put the lid on and cook on High for 2 hours.
2. Divide between plates and serve as a side dish.

per serving: 63 calories,1.5g protein, 6.2g carbohydrates, 3.8g fat, 2.5g fiber, 0mg cholesterol, 7mg sodium, 278mg potassium.

Garlic Mix

Preparation time: 10 minutes
Cooking time: 4 hours
Servings: 2

Ingredients:
- 1 pound carrots, sliced
- 2 garlic cloves, minced
- 1 red onion, chopped
- 1 tablespoon olive oil
- ½ cup tomato sauce
- ½ teaspoon oregano, dried
- 2 teaspoons lemon zest, grated
- 1 tablespoon lemon juice
- 1 tablespoon chives, chopped

Directions:
1. In your slow cooker, mix the carrots with the garlic, onion, and the other ingredients, toss, put the lid on and cook on Low for 4 hours.
2. Divide the mix between plates and serve.

per serving: 199 calories,3.7g protein, 32.6g carbohydrates, 7.3g fat, 8.1g fiber, 0mg cholesterol, 482mg sodium, 1046mg potassium.

Curry Mix

Preparation time: 10 minutes
Cooking time: 3 hours
Servings: 2

Ingredients:

- 1-pound broccoli florets
- 1 cup tomato paste
- 1 tablespoon red curry paste
- 1 red onion, sliced
- ½ teaspoon Italian seasoning
- 1 teaspoon thyme, dried
- ½ tablespoon cilantro, chopped

Directions:

1. In your slow cooker, mix the broccoli with the curry paste, tomato paste, and the other ingredients, toss, put the lid on and cook on Low for 3 hours.
2. Divide the mix between plates and serve as a side dish.

per serving: 238 calories,12.7g protein, 46.8g carbohydrates, 3.7g fat, 12.7g fiber, 0mg cholesterol, 596mg sodium, 2132mg potassium.

Cauliflower Mix

Preparation time: 10 minutes
Cooking time: 4 hours
Servings: 2

Ingredients:

- 1 cup cauliflower florets
- ½ pound sweet potatoes, peeled and cubed
- 1 cup vegetable stock
- ½ cup tomato sauce
- 1 tablespoon chives, chopped
- 1 teaspoon sweet paprika

Directions:

1. In your slow cooker, mix the cauliflower with the potatoes, stock, and the other ingredients, toss, put the lid on and cook on High for 4 hours.
2. Divide between plates and serve as a side dish.

per serving: 174 calories,4.2g protein, 40.2g carbohydrates, 0.5g fat, 7.8g fiber, 0mg cholesterol, 417mg sodium, 1374mg potassium.

Asparagus and Parsley Mix

Preparation time: 10 minutes
Cooking time: 2 hours
Servings: 2

Ingredients:
- 1-pound asparagus, trimmed and halved
- 1 red onion, sliced
- 2 garlic cloves, minced
- 1 cup vegetable stock
- 1 tablespoon lemon juice
- ¼ cup parsley, chopped

Directions:
1. In your slow cooker, mix the asparagus with the onion, garlic, and the other ingredients, toss, put the lid on and cook on High for 2 hours.
2. Divide between plates and serve as a side dish.

per serving: 86 calories, 6.6g protein, 17.6g carbohydrates, 0.5g fat, 6.8g fiber, 0mg cholesterol, 86mg sodium, 666mg potassium.

Turmeric Squash Mix

Preparation time: 10 minutes
Cooking time: 3 hours
Servings: 2

Ingredients:
- 1 pound butternut squash, peeled and cubed
- 2 spring onions, chopped
- 1 cup vegetable stock
- ½ teaspoon red pepper flakes, crushed
- ½ teaspoon turmeric powder
- 3 garlic cloves, minced

Directions:
1. In your slow cooker, mix the squash with the garlic, stock, and the other ingredients, toss, put the lid on and cook on Low for 3 hours.
2. Divide squash mix between plates and serve as a side dish.

per serving: 127 calories, 3.4g protein, 31.7g carbohydrates, 0.4g fat, 5.8g fiber, 0mg cholesterol, 83mg sodium, 946mg potassium.

Baby Carrots Mix

Preparation time: 10 minutes
Cooking time: 6 hours
Servings: 2

Ingredients:

- 1 tablespoon avocado oil
- 1 pound baby carrots, peeled
- ½ pound parsnips, peeled and cut into sticks
- 1 teaspoon sweet paprika
- ½ cup tomato paste
- ½ cup vegetable stock
- ½ teaspoon chili powder
- 2 garlic cloves, minced
- 1 tablespoon dill, chopped

Directions:

1. Grease the slow cooker with the oil and mix the carrots with the parsnips, paprika, and the other ingredients inside.
2. Toss, put the lid on, and cook on Low for 6 hours.
3. Divide everything between plates and serve as a side dish.

per serving: 246 calories,6.7g protein, 55.7g carbohydrates, 2.2g fat, 16.3g fiber, 0mg cholesterol, 298mg sodium, 1783mg potassium.

Brussels Sprouts Bowls with Ginger Powder

Preparation time: 10 minutes
Cooking time: 4 hours
Servings: 2

Ingredients:

- 1 cup Brussels sprouts, trimmed and halved
- 1 cup cauliflower florets
- 1 tablespoon olive oil
- 1 cup vegetable stock
- 2 tablespoons tomato paste
- 1 teaspoon chili powder
- ½ teaspoon ginger powder
- 1 tablespoon thyme, chopped

Directions:

1. In your slow cooker, mix the Brussels sprouts with the cauliflower, oil, stock, and the other ingredients, toss, put the lid on and cook on Low for 4 hours.
2. Divide the mix between plates and serve as a side dish.

per serving: 124 calories,4g protein, 13.6g carbohydrates, 7.6g fat, 5.1g fiber, 0mg cholesterol, 126mg sodium, 592mg potassium.

Cabbage and Spices Bowls

Preparation time: 10 minutes
Cooking time: 2 hours
Servings: 2

Ingredients:

- 1 red onion, sliced
- 1 cup green cabbage, shredded
- 1 cup baby kale
- ½ cup canned tomatoes, crushed
- ½ teaspoon hot paprika
- ½ teaspoon Italian seasoning
- 1 tablespoon dill, chopped

Directions:

1. In your slow cooker, mix the cabbage with the kale, onion, and the other ingredients, toss, put the lid on and cook on High for 2 hours.
2. Divide between plates and serve right away as a side dish.

per serving: 69 calories,3.3g protein, 14.4g carbohydrates, 0.9g fat, 3.8g fiber, 1mg cholesterol, 32mg sodium, 298mg potassium.

Basil Kale Mix

Preparation time: 10 minutes
Cooking time: 2 hours
Servings: 2

Ingredients:

- 1 yellow bell pepper, chopped
- 1 red bell pepper, chopped
- 1 tablespoon olive oil
- 1 red onion, sliced
- 4 cups baby kale
- 1 teaspoon lemon zest, grated
- 1 tablespoon lemon juice
- ½ cup vegetable stock
- 1 garlic clove, minced
- 1 tablespoon basil, chopped

Directions:

1. In your slow cooker, mix the kale with the oil, onion, bell peppers, and the other ingredients, toss, put the lid on, and cook on Low for 2 hours.
2. Divide the mix between plates and serve as a side dish.

per serving: 178 calories,6.6g protein, 24.9g carbohydrates, 7.5g fat, 4.2g fiber, 0mg cholesterol, 114mg sodium, 825mg potassium.

Thyme Corn

Preparation time: 10 minutes
Cooking time: 4 hours
Servings: 2

Ingredients:
- 4 garlic cloves, minced
- 1 tablespoon olive oil
- 1 pound white mushroom caps, halved
- 1 cup of corn kernels
- 1 cup canned tomatoes, crushed
- ¼ teaspoon thyme, dried
- ½ cup vegetable stock
- 2 tablespoons parsley, chopped

Directions:
1. Grease your slow cooker with the oil, and mix the garlic with the mushrooms, corn, and the other ingredients inside.
2. Toss, put the lid on, and cook on Low for 4 hours.
3. Divide between plates and serve as a side dish.

per serving: 168 calories,5.5g protein, 22.8g carbohydrates, 8.2g fat, 4.2g fiber, 0mg cholesterol, 62mg sodium, 650mg potassium.

Paprika Green Beans

Preparation time: 10 minutes
Cooking time: 3 hours
Servings: 2

Ingredients:
- 1 pound green beans, trimmed and halved
- 1 cup zucchinis, cubed
- 1 cup tomato sauce
- 1 teaspoon smoked paprika
- ½ teaspoon cumin, ground
- ½ teaspoon garlic powder
- ¼ tablespoon chives, chopped

Directions:
1. In your slow cooker, mix the green beans with the zucchinis, tomato sauce, and the other ingredients, toss, put the lid on and cook on Low for 3 hours.
2. Divide the mix between plates and serve as a side dish.

per serving: 116 calories,6.8g protein, 26g carbohydrates, 0.9g fat, 10.7g fiber, 0mg cholesterol, 663mg sodium, 1070mg potassium.

Vinegar Sweet Potatoes

Preparation time: 10 minutes
Cooking time: 3 hours
Servings: 4

Ingredients:

- 1 pound sweet potatoes, peeled and cut into wedges
- 1 cup vegetable stock
- ½ teaspoon chili powder
- ½ teaspoon cumin, ground
- 1 tablespoon olive oil
- 1 tablespoon tarragon, dried
- 2 tablespoons balsamic vinegar

Directions:

1. In your slow cooker, mix the sweet potatoes with the stock, chili powder, and the other ingredients, toss, put the lid on and cook on High for 3 hours.
2. Divide the mix between plates and serve as a side dish.

per serving: 174 calories,2.2g protein, 33.2g carbohydrates, 3.8g fat, 5.1g fiber, 0mg cholesterol, 50mg sodium, 988mg potassium.

Mustard and balsamic Vinegar Brussels Sprouts

Preparation time: 10 minutes
Cooking time: 3 hours
Servings: 2

Ingredients:

- 1 pound Brussels sprouts, trimmed and halved
- 1 tablespoon olive oil
- 1 tablespoon mustard
- 1 tablespoon balsamic vinegar
- ¼ cup vegetable stock
- A pinch of red pepper, crushed
- 2 tablespoons chives, chopped

Directions:

1. In your slow cooker, mix the Brussels sprouts with the oil, mustard, and the other ingredients, toss, put the lid on and cook on High for 3 hours.
2. Divide the mix between plates and serve as a side dish.

per serving: 189 calories,9.4g protein, 23.3g carbohydrates, 9.4g fat, 9.5g fiber, 0mg cholesterol, 75mg sodium, 950mg potassium.

Parmesan Greens

Preparation time: 10 minutes
Cooking time: 2 hours
Servings: 2

Ingredients:
- 2 garlic cloves, minced
- 1 pound baby spinach
- ¼ cup vegetable stock
- A drizzle of olive oil
- 4 tablespoons Greek-style yogurt
- 2 tablespoons parmesan cheese, grated

Directions:
1. Grease your Crockpot with the oil, and mix the spinach with the garlic and the other ingredients inside.
2. Toss, put the lid on, and cook on Low for 2 hours.
3. Divide the mix between plates and serve as a side dish.

per serving: 149 calories,15.8g protein, 10.7g carbohydrates, 6.9g fat, 5.2g fiber, 20mg cholesterol, 457mg sodium, 1294mg potassium.

Minty Tomatoes

Preparation time: 10 minutes
Cooking time: 3 hours
Servings: 2

Ingredients:
- 1 pound okra, sliced
- ½ pound tomatoes, cut into wedges
- 1 tablespoon olive oil
- ½ cup vegetable stock
- ½ teaspoon chili powder
- 1 tablespoon mint, chopped
- 3 green onions, chopped
- 1 tablespoon chives, chopped

Directions:
1. Grease your slow cooker with the oil, and mix the okra with the tomatoes and the other ingredients inside.
2. Put the lid on, cook on Low for 3 hours, divide between plates, and serve as a side dish.

per serving: 187 calories,6.3g protein, 24.6g carbohydrates, 7.8g fat, 9.9g fiber, 0mg cholesterol, 68mg sodium, 1071mg potassium.

Savoy Cabbage and Sweet Paprika Bowls

Preparation time: 10 minutes
Cooking time: 2 hours
Servings: 2

Ingredients:

- 1 pound Savoy cabbage, shredded
- 1 red onion, sliced
- 1 tablespoon olive oil
- ½ cup vegetable stock
- 1 carrot, grated
- ½ cup tomatoes, cubed
- ½ teaspoon sweet paprika
- ½ inch ginger, grated

Directions:

1. In your slow cooker, mix the cabbage with the onion, oil, and the other ingredients, toss, put the lid on and cook on High for 2 hours.
2. Divide the mix between plates and serve as a side dish.

per serving: 167 calories,4.5g protein, 24.7g carbohydrates, 7.5g fat, 8.7g fiber, 0mg cholesterol, 102mg sodium, 721mg potassium.

Dill Cauliflower

Preparation time: 10 minutes
Cooking time: 5 hours
Servings: 2

Ingredients:

- 2 cups cauliflower florets
- ½ cup vegetable stock
- 1 tablespoon balsamic vinegar
- 1 tablespoon lemon zest, grated
- 2 spring onions, chopped
- ¼ teaspoon sweet paprika
- 1 tablespoon dill, chopped

Directions:

1. In your slow cooker, mix the cauliflower with the stock, vinegar, and the other ingredients, toss, put the lid on, and cook on Low for 5 hours.
2. Divide the cauliflower mix between plates and serve.

per serving: 43 calories,2.9g protein, 9.1g carbohydrates, 0.3g fat, 0.6g fiber, 0mg cholesterol, 71mg sodium, 449mg potassium.

Italian Black Beans and Celery Bowls

Preparation time: 10 minutes
Cooking time: 5 hours
Servings: 4

Ingredients:
- 2 tablespoons tomato paste
- 2 cups black beans
- ¼ cup vegetable stock
- 1 red onion, sliced
- Cooking spray
- 1 teaspoon Italian seasoning
- ½ celery rib, chopped
- ½ red bell pepper, chopped
- ½ sweet red pepper, chopped
- ¼ teaspoon mustard seeds
- 1 tablespoon cilantro, chopped

Directions:
1. Grease the slow cooker with the cooking spray, and mix the beans with the stock, onion, and the other ingredients inside.
2. Put the lid on, cook on Low for 5 hours, divide between plates, and serve as a side dish.

per serving: 360 calories, 21.9g protein, 66.3g carbohydrates, 1.9g fat, 16g fiber, 66.3mg cholesterol, 27mg sodium, 1612mg potassium.

Sage Peas with Garlic

Preparation time: 10 minutes
Cooking time: 2 hours
Servings: 2

Ingredients:
- 1 pound peas
- 1 red onion, sliced
- ½ cup vegetable stock
- ½ cup tomato sauce
- 2 garlic cloves, minced
- ¼ teaspoon sage, dried
- 1 tablespoon dill, chopped

Directions:
1. In your slow cooker, combine the peas with the onion, stock, and the other ingredients, toss, put the lid on and cook on Low for 2 hours.
2. Divide between plates and serve as a side dish.

per serving: 234 calories, 14.5g protein, 44.1g carbohydrates, 1.2g fat, 14.2g fiber, 0mg cholesterol, 373mg sodium, 933mg potassium.

Dill Mushroom Stew

Preparation time: 10 minutes
Cooking time: 3 hours
Servings: 2

Ingredients:

- 1 pound white mushrooms, halved
- 1 tablespoon olive oil
- 1 red onion, sliced
- 1 carrot, peeled and grated
- 2 green onions, chopped
- 1 garlic clove, minced
- 1 cup beef stock
- ½ cup tomato sauce
- 1 tablespoon dill, chopped

Directions:

1. Grease the slow cooker with the oil and mix the mushrooms with the onion, carrot, and the other ingredients inside.
2. Put the lid on, cook on Low for 3 hours, divide between plates, and serve as a side dish.

per serving: 177 calories,10.8g protein, 21.4g carbohydrates, 8.2g fat, 5.8g fiber, 0mg cholesterol, 794mg sodium, 1265mg potassium.

Ginger Zucchini Mix

Preparation time: 10 minutes
Cooking time: 2 hours
Servings: 2

Ingredients:

- ¼ cup carrots, grated
- 1 pound zucchinis, roughly cubed
- 1 teaspoon hot paprika
- ½ teaspoon chili powder
- 2 spring onions, chopped
- ½ tablespoon olive oil
- ½ teaspoon curry powder
- 1 garlic clove, minced
- ½ teaspoon ginger powder
- 1 tablespoon cilantro, chopped

Directions:

1. In your slow cooker, mix the carrots with the zucchinis, paprika, and the other ingredients, toss, put the lid on and cook on Low for 2 hours.
2. Divide between plates and serve as a side dish.

per serving: 84 calories,3.4g protein, 11.5g carbohydrates, 4.2g fat, 3.7g fiber, 0mg cholesterol, 42mg sodium, 714mg potassium.

Carrots and Pistachios Mix

Preparation time: 10 minutes
Cooking time: 2 hours
Servings: 2

Ingredients:

- 2 carrots, sliced
- 1 small yellow onion, chopped
- ¼ teaspoon oregano, dried
- ½ teaspoon sweet paprika
- 2 ounces baby spinach
- 1 cup vegetable stock
- 1 tablespoon lemon juice
- 2 tablespoons pistachios, chopped

Directions:

1. In your slow cooker, mix the spinach with the carrots, onion, and the other ingredients, toss, put the lid on, and cook on Low for 2 hours.
2. Divide everything between plates and serve.

per serving: 79 calories, 3.1g protein, 13.9g carbohydrates, 2.1g fat, 4.1g fiber, 0mg cholesterol, 198mg sodium, 533mg potassium.

Creamy Sweet Potatoes

Preparation time: 10 minutes
Cooking time: 4 hours
Servings: 2

Ingredients:

- ½ pound sweet potatoes, halved and sliced
- 2 scallions, chopped
- 1 tablespoon avocado oil
- 2 ounces of coconut milk
- ¼ cup vegetable stock
- 1 tablespoons parsley, chopped

Directions:

1. In your slow cooker, mix the potatoes with the scallions and the other ingredients, toss, put the lid on and cook on High for 4 hours.
2. Divide the mix between plates and serve.

per serving: 216 calories, 2.9g protein, 35.3g carbohydrates, 7.9g fat, 6.2g fiber, 0mg cholesterol, 36mg sodium, 1090mg potassium.

Sage and Orange Sweet Potatoes

Preparation time: 10 minutes
Cooking time: 3 hours
Servings: 2

Ingredients:
- ½ pound sweet potatoes, thinly sliced
- 1 tablespoon sage, chopped
- 2 tablespoons orange juice
- ½ cup vegetable stock
- ½ tablespoon olive oil

Directions:
1. In your slow cooker, mix the potatoes with the sage and the other ingredients, toss, put the lid on and cook on High for 3 hours.
2. Divide between plates and serve as a side dish.

per serving: 175 calories, 2.1g protein, 34.1g carbohydrates, 3.9g fat, 5.2g fiber, 0mg cholesterol, 23mg sodium, 967mg potassium.

Cauliflower and Almonds Bowls

Preparation time: 10 minutes
Cooking time: 3 hours
Servings: 2

Ingredients:
- 2 cups cauliflower florets
- 2 ounces tomato paste
- 1 small yellow onion, chopped
- 1 tablespoon chives, chopped
- 1 tablespoon almonds, sliced

Directions:
1. In your slow cooker, mix the cauliflower with the tomato paste and the other ingredients, toss, put the lid on and cook on High for 3 hours.
2. Divide between plates and serve as a side dish.

per serving: 80 calories, 4.3g protein, 14.6g carbohydrates, 1.8g fat, 4.8g fiber, 0mg cholesterol, 59mg sodium, 668mg potassium.

Fragrant Risotto

Preparation time: 10 minutes
Cooking time: 2 hours
Servings: 2

Ingredients:
- 1 small shallot, chopped
- 1 cup of brown rice
- 1 cup chicken stock
- 1 tablespoon olive oil
- 2 garlic cloves, minced
- 2 tablespoons cilantro, chopped

Directions:
1. In your slow cooker, mix the rice with the stock, shallot, and the other ingredients, toss, put the lid on and cook on High for 2 hours
2. Divide between plates and serve as a side dish.

per serving: 417 calories,7.8g protein, 74.6g carbohydrates, 9.9g fat, 3.3g fiber, 0mg cholesterol, 387mg sodium,296mg potassium.

Curry Vegetable Mix

Preparation time: 10 minutes
Cooking time: 3 hours
Servings: 2

Ingredients:
- 2 zucchinis, cubed
- 1 eggplant, cubed
- ½ cup button mushrooms, quartered
- 1 small sweet potato, chopped
- ½ cup vegetable stock
- 1 garlic cloves, minced
- ¼ tablespoon Thai red curry paste
- ¼ tablespoon ginger, grated
- 2 tablespoons coconut milk

Directions:
1. In your slow cooker, mix the zucchinis with the eggplant and the other ingredients, toss, put the lid on and cook on Low for 3 hours.
2. Divide between plates and serve as a side dish.

per serving: 2185 calories,6.3g protein, 33.5g carbohydrates, 5.1g fat, 12.5g fiber, 0mg cholesterol, 141mg sodium, 1454mg potassium.

Rosemary Leeks with tomato Sauce

Preparation time: 10 minutes
Cooking time: 3 hours
Servings: 2

Ingredients:
- ½ tablespoon olive oil
- ½ leeks, sliced
- ½ cup tomato sauce
- 2 garlic cloves, minced
- ¼ tablespoon rosemary, chopped

Directions:
1. In your slow cooker, mix the leeks with the oil, sauce, and the other ingredients, toss, put the lid on, cook on High for 3 hours, divide between plates and serve as a side dish.

per serving: 64 calories,1.4g protein, 7.7g carbohydrates, 3.8g fat, 1.6g fiber, 0mg cholesterol, 326mg sodium, 259mg potassium.

Cherry Tomatoes Medley

Preparation time: 10 minutes
Cooking time: 3 hours
Servings: 2

Ingredients:
- 1 zucchini, cubed
- 1 eggplant, cubed
- ½ cup baby carrots, peeled
- ½ cup baby kale
- 1 cup cherry tomatoes, halved
- 1 teaspoon sweet paprika
- 1 tablespoon olive oil
- 1 cup tomato sauce
- 1 teaspoon Italian seasoning
- 1 cup yellow squash, peeled and cut into wedges
- 1 teaspoon garlic powder
- 1 tablespoon cilantro, chopped

Directions:
1. Grease your Crockpot with the oil, and mix the zucchini with the eggplant, carrots, and the other ingredients inside.
2. Toss, put the lid on, and cook on Low for 3 hours.
3. Divide the mix between plates and serve as a side dish.

per serving: 206 calories,7g protein, 31.2g carbohydrates, 9g fat, 13.2g fiber, 2mg cholesterol, 673mg sodium, 1450mg potassium.

Maple Syrup Brussels Sprouts

Preparation time: 10 minutes
Cooking time: 3 hours
Servings: 2

Ingredients:

- ½ pounds Brussels sprouts, trimmed and halved
- 2 tablespoons mustard
- ½ cup vegetable stock
- 1 tablespoon olive oil
- 2 tablespoons maple syrup
- 1 tablespoon thyme, chopped

Directions:

1. In your slow cooker, mix the sprouts with the mustard and the other ingredients, toss, put the lid on and cook on Low for 3 hours. Divide between plates and serve as a side dish.

per serving: 219 calories,6.9g protein, 28.7g carbohydrates, 10.8g fat, 6.5g fiber, 0mg cholesterol, 44mg sodium, 569mg potassium.

Rice with Vegetables

Preparation time: 6 minutes
Cooking time: 5 hours
Servings: 4

Ingredients:

- 2 cups brown rice
- 1 cup mixed carrots, peas, corn, and green beans
- 2 cups of water
- ½ teaspoon green chili
- ½ teaspoon ginger, grated
- 3 garlic cloves, minced
- 2 tablespoons pumpkin puree
- 1 cinnamon stick
- 1 tablespoon cumin seeds
- 2 bay leaves
- 3 whole cloves
- 5 black peppercorns
- 2 whole cardamoms
- 1 tablespoon honey

Directions:

1. Put the water in your Slow cooker, add rice, mixed veggies, green chili, grated ginger, garlic, cinnamon stick, whole cloves, pumpkin puree, cumin seeds, bay leaves, cardamoms, black peppercorns, and honey, stir, cover, and cook on Low for 5 hours. Discard the cinnamon, divide between plates and serve as a side dish.

per serving: 388 calories,8.2g protein, 81.7g carbohydrates, 2.9g fat, 3.7g fiber, 0mg cholesterol, 19mg sodium, 315mg potassium.

Cilantro Black Beans Mix

Preparation time: 10 minutes
Cooking time: 6 hours
Servings: 2

Ingredients:

- ½ pound black beans, soaked overnight and drained
- ½ cup vegetable stock
- ½ tablespoon lime juice
- 2 tablespoons cilantro, chopped
- 2 tablespoons pine nuts

Directions:

1. In your slow cooker, mix the beans with the stock and the other ingredients, toss, put the lid on and cook on Low for 6 hours.
2. Divide everything between plates and serve.

per serving: 446 calories,25.8g protein, 72.1g carbohydrates, 7.5g fat, 17.7g fiber, 0mg cholesterol, 19mg sodium, 1738mg potassium.

Goat Cheese Rice with Spinach

Preparation time: 10 minutes
Cooking time: 4 hours
Servings: 6

Ingredients:

- 2 garlic cloves, minced
- 2 tablespoons olive oil
- ¾ cup yellow onion, chopped
- 1 ½ cups brown rice
- 12 ounces spinach, chopped
- 3 ½ cups vegetable stock
- 4 ounces goat cheese, soft and crumbled
- 2 tablespoons lemon juice
- 1/3 cup pecans, toasted and chopped

Directions:

1. In your Slow cooker, mix oil with garlic, onion, rice, and stock, stir, cover, and cook on Low for 4 hours.
2. Add spinach, toss and leave aside for a few minutes
3. Add lemon juice and goat cheese, stir, divide between plates and serve with pecans on top as a side dish.

per serving: 371 calories,12.2g protein, 42g carbohydrates, 18g fat, 4.3g fiber, 20mg cholesterol, 143mg sodium, 513mg potassium.

Fish and Seafood

Garam Masala Mackerel

Preparation time: 5 minutes
Cooking time: 3 hours
Servings: 4

Ingredients:
- 1-pound mackerel fillets, boneless, skinless, and cubed
- 1 tablespoon avocado oil
- 1 cup coconut cream
- ½ teaspoon cumin, ground
- 2 scallions, chopped
- ½ teaspoon garam masala
- 1 tablespoon cilantro, chopped

Directions:
1. In your slow cooker, mix the mackerel with the oil, cream, and the other ingredients, toss, put the lid on and cook on Low for 3 hours.
2. Divide the mix into bowls and serve.

per serving: 443 calories,28.7g protein, 4.2g carbohydrates, 3.5g fat, 1.7g fiber, 85mg cholesterol, 106mg sodium, 650mg potassium.

Lemon Salmon with Peas

Preparation time: 10 minutes
Cooking time: 2 hours
Servings: 2

Ingredients:
- 1-pound salmon fillets, boneless and cubed
- 1 tablespoon olive oil
- 1 cup sugar snap peas
- 1 tablespoon lemon juice
- ½ cup tomato passata
- 1 tablespoon chives, chopped

Directions:
1. In your slow cooker, mix the salmon with the peas, oil, and the other ingredients, toss, put the lid on and cook on High for 2 hours.
2. Divide the mix between plates and serve.

per serving: 383 calories,45.3g protein, 4.2g carbohydrates, 21.2g fat, 0.9g fiber, 100mg cholesterol, 103mg sodium, 948mg potassium.

Chili Shrimp with Scallions

Preparation time: 10 minutes
Cooking time: 1 hour
Servings: 4

Ingredients:
- 1-pound shrimp, peeled and deveined
- 1 zucchini, cubed
- 2 scallions, minced
- 1 cup tomato passata
- 2 green chilies, chopped
- 1 tablespoon chives, chopped

Directions:
1. In your slow cooker, mix the shrimp with the zucchini and the other ingredients, toss, put the lid on and cook on High for 1 hour.
2. Divide the shrimp mix into bowls and serve.

per serving: 154 calories,27g protein, 5.7g carbohydrates, 2.1g fat, 0.8g fiber, 239mg cholesterol, 283mg sodium, 348mg potassium.

Italian Shrimp with Chives

Preparation time: 5 minutes
Cooking time: 1 hour
Servings: 2

Ingredients:
- 1-pound shrimp, peeled and deveined
- 1 tablespoon avocado oil
- ½ teaspoon sweet paprika
- 1 teaspoon Italian seasoning
- Juice of 1 lime
- ¼ cup chicken stock
- 1 tablespoon chives, chopped

Directions:
1. In your slow cooker, mix the shrimp with the oil, seasoning, and the other ingredients, toss, put the lid on and cook on High for 1 hour.
2. Divide the mix into bowls and serve.

per serving: 289 calories,52g protein, 4.6g carbohydrates, 5.6g fat, 0.6g fiber, 479mg cholesterol, 650mg sodium, 426mg potassium.

Basil Cod

Preparation time: 5 minutes
Cooking time: 3 hours
Servings: 4

Ingredients:

- 1-pound cod fillets, boneless
- 1 cup black olives, pitted and halved
- ½ tablespoon tomato paste
- 1 tablespoon basil, chopped
- ¼ cup chicken stock
- 1 red onion, sliced
- 1 tablespoon lime juice
- 1 tablespoon chives, chopped

Directions:

1. In your slow cooker, mix the cod with the olives, basil, and the other ingredients, toss, put the lid on and cook on Low for 3 hours.
2. Divide everything between plates and serve.

per serving: 142 calories,20.8g protein, 5.2g carbohydrates, 4.7g fat, 1.8g fiber, 55mg cholesterol, 414mg sodium, 68mg potassium.

Tuna and Onion Mix

Preparation time: 10 minutes
Cooking time: 2 hours
Servings: 4

Ingredients:

- 1-pound tuna fillets, boneless and cubed
- 1 fennel bulb, sliced
- ½ cup chicken stock
- ½ teaspoon sweet paprika
- ½ teaspoon chili powder
- 1 red onion, chopped
- 2 tablespoons cilantro, chopped

Directions:

1. In your slow cooker, mix the tuna with the fennel, stock, and the other ingredients, toss, put the lid on and cook on High for 2 hours.
2. Divide the mix between plates and serve.

per serving: 395 calories,22.2g protein, 7.3g carbohydrates, 31.1g fat, 2.6g fiber, 0mg cholesterol, 131mg sodium, 300mg potassium.

Shrimp and Mushrooms Saute

Preparation time: 10 minutes
Cooking time: 1 hour
Servings: 2

Ingredients:

- 1-pound shrimp, peeled and deveined
- 1 cup white mushrooms, halved
- 1 tablespoon avocado oil
- ½ tablespoon tomato paste
- 4 scallions, minced
- ½ cup chicken stock
- Juice of 1 lime
- 1 tablespoon chives, minced

Directions:

1. In your slow cooker, mix the shrimp with the mushrooms, oil, and the other ingredients, toss, put the lid on and cook on High for 1 hour.
2. Divide the mix into bowls and serve.

per serving: 302 calories, 53.8g protein, 8.2g carbohydrates, 5.1g fat, 1.6g fiber, 478mg cholesterol, 755mg sodium, 649mg potassium.

Salmon with Berries

Preparation time: 10 minutes
Cooking time: 3 hours
Servings: 4

Ingredients:

- 1 pound salmon fillets, boneless and roughly cubed
- ½ cup blackberries
- Juice of 1 lime
- 1 tablespoon avocado oil
- 2 scallions, chopped
- ½ teaspoon Italian seasoning
- ½ cup fish stock

Directions:

1. In your slow cooker, mix the salmon with the berries, lime juice, and the other ingredients, toss, put the lid on and cook on Low for 3 hours.
2. Divide the mix between plates and serve.

per serving: 172 calories, 23.1g protein, 2.5g carbohydrates, 8g fat, 1.3g fiber, 51mg cholesterol, 97mg sodium, 539mg potassium.

Cod with Vegetables

Preparation time: 5 minutes
Cooking time: 3 hours
Servings: 4

Ingredients:
- 1-pound cod fillets, boneless and roughly cubed
- 1 cup artichoke hearts, cooked and quartered
- 2 scallions, chopped
- 1 tablespoon olive oil
- ½ cup chicken stock
- 1 tablespoon lime juice
- 1 tablespoon cilantro, chopped

Directions:
1. In your slow cooker, mix the cod with the artichokes, scallions, and the other ingredients, toss, put the lid on and cook on Low for 3 hours.
2. Divide the mix between plates and serve.

per serving: 144 calories,21.6g protein, 5.4g carbohydrates, 4.7g fat, 2.4g fiber, 55mg cholesterol, 206mg sodium, 179mg potassium.

Salmon and Green Beans

Preparation time: 5 minutes
Cooking time: 2 hours
Servings: 4

Ingredients:
- 1-pound salmon fillets, boneless and cubed
- 1 cup cherry tomatoes, halved
- 1 cup green beans, trimmed and halved
- 1 cup tomato passata
- ½ cup chicken stock
- 1 tablespoon parsley, chopped

Directions:
1. In your slow cooker, mix the salmon with the tomatoes, green beans, and the other ingredients, toss, put the lid on and cook on High for 2 hours.
2. Divide the mix into bowls and serve.

per serving: 183 calories,23.7g protein, 7g carbohydrates, 7.3g fat, 1.5g fiber, 50mg cholesterol, 150mg sodium, 607mg potassium.

Coriander Shrimp Bowls

Preparation time: 5 minutes
Cooking time: 1 hour and 30 minutes
Servings: 4

Ingredients:

- 1-pound shrimp, peeled and deveined
- 1 cup chicken stock
- ½ cup wild rice
- ½ cup carrots, peeled and cubed
- 1 green bell pepper, cubed
- ½ teaspoon turmeric powder
- ½ teaspoon coriander, ground
- 1 tablespoon olive oil
- 1 red onion, chopped
- 1 tablespoon cilantro, chopped

Directions:

1. In your slow cooker, mix the stock with the rice, carrots, and the other ingredients except for the shrimp, toss, put the lid on and cook on High for 1 hour.
2. Add the shrimp, toss, put the lid back on and cook on High for 30 minutes.
3. Divide the mix between plates and serve.

per serving: 266 calories,29.7g protein, 23.3g carbohydrates, 5.9g fat, 2.6g fiber, 239mg cholesterol, 480mg sodium, 429mg potassium.

Rosemary Mussels

Preparation time: 5 minutes
Cooking time: 1 hour
Servings: 4

Ingredients:

- 1 pound mussels, debearded
- ½ teaspoon coriander, ground
- ½ teaspoon rosemary, dried
- 1 tablespoon lime zest, grated
- Juice of 1 lime
- 1 cup tomato passata
- ¼ cup chicken stock
- 1 tablespoon chives, chopped

Directions:

1. In your slow cooker, mix the mussels with the coriander, rosemary, and the other ingredients, toss, put the lid on and cook on High for 1 hour. Divide the mix into bowls and serve.

per serving: 107 calories,13.9g protein, 6.2g carbohydrates, 2.6g fat, 0.2g fiber, 32mg cholesterol, 372mg sodium, 370mg potassium.

Chives Calamari

Preparation time: 10 minutes
Cooking time: 2 hours
Servings: 2

Ingredients:
- 1 pound calamari rings
- 2 scallions, chopped
- 2 garlic cloves, minced
- ½ cup Greek-style yogurt
- ½ cup chicken stock
- 1 tablespoon lime juice
- ½ cup black olives pitted and halved
- 2 tablespoons chives, chopped

Directions:
1. In your slow cooker, mix the calamari with the scallions, garlic, and the other ingredients except for the yogurt, toss, put the lid on and cook on High for 1 hour. Add the yogurt, toss, cook on High for 1 more hour, divide into bowls and serve.

per serving: 170 calories,10.8g protein, 14.9g carbohydrates, 7.6g fat, 0.6g fiber, 4mg cholesterol, 240mg sodium, 165mg potassium.

Salmon and Tomatoes Salad

Preparation time: 5 minutes
Cooking time: 3 hours
Servings: 4

Ingredients:
- 1 pound salmon fillets, boneless and cubed
- ¼ cup chicken stock
- 1 zucchini, cut with a spiralizer
- 1 carrot, sliced
- 1 eggplant, cubed
- ½ cup cherry tomatoes halved
- 1 red onion, sliced
- ½ teaspoon turmeric powder
- ½ teaspoon chili powder
- ½ tablespoon rosemary, chopped
- 1 tablespoon chives, chopped

Directions:
1. In your slow cooker, mix the salmon with the zucchini, stock, carrot, and the other ingredients, toss, put the lid on and cook on High for 3 hours.
2. Divide the mix into bowls and serve.

per serving: 208 calories,24.3g protein, 13.1g carbohydrates, 7.5g fat, 5.9g fiber, 50mg cholesterol, 120mg sodium, 935mg potassium.

Parsley and Walnut Tuna Mix

Preparation time: 10 minutes
Cooking time: 3 hours
Servings: 4

Ingredients:
- 1 pound tuna fillets, boneless
- ½ tablespoon walnuts, chopped
- ½ cup chicken stock
- ½ teaspoon chili powder
- ½ teaspoon sweet paprika
- 1 red onion, sliced
- 2 tablespoons parsley, chopped

Directions:
1. In your slow cooker, mix the tuna with the walnuts, stock, and the other ingredients, toss, put the lid on and cook on High for 3 hours.
2. Divide everything between plates and serve.

per serving: 384 calories, 21.4g protein, 3.2g carbohydrates, 31.8g fat, 0.9g fiber, 0mg cholesterol, 101mg sodium, 70mg potassium.

Almond Shrimp with Cabbage

Preparation time: 5 minutes
Cooking time: 1 hour
Servings: 4

Ingredients:
- 1 pound shrimp, peeled and deveined
- 1 cup red cabbage, shredded
- 1 tablespoon almonds, chopped
- 1 cup cherry tomatoes, halved
- 1 tablespoon balsamic vinegar
- 2 tablespoons olive oil
- ½ cup tomato passata

Directions:
1. In your slow cooker, mix the shrimp with the cabbage, almonds, and the other ingredients, toss, put the lid on and cook on High for 1 hour.
2. Divide everything into bowls and serve.

per serving: 220 calories, 26.9g protein, 5.6g carbohydrates, 9.8g fat, 1.2g fiber, 239mg cholesterol, 282mg sodium, 342mg potassium.

Shrimp and Kale Garnish

Preparation time: 5 minutes
Cooking time: 1 hour
Servings: 2

Ingredients:

- 1 pound shrimp, peeled and deveined
- ½ cup cherry tomatoes halved
- 1 cup baby kale
- ½ cup chicken stock
- 1 tablespoon olive oil
- Juice of 1 lime
- ½ teaspoon sweet paprika
- 1 tablespoon cilantro, chopped

Directions:

1. In your slow cooker, mix the shrimp with the cherry tomatoes, kale, and the other ingredients, toss, put the lid on and cook on High for 1 hour.
2. Divide the mix into bowls and serve.

per serving: 360 calories,53.7g protein, 9.2g carbohydrates, 11.4g fat, 1.5g fiber, 478mg cholesterol, 768mg sodium, 403mg potassium.

Trout Bowls with Olives

Preparation time: 5 minutes
Cooking time: 3 hours
Servings: 4

Ingredients:

- 1-pound trout fillets, boneless, skinless, and cubed
- 1 cup kalamata olives, pitted and chopped
- 1 cup baby spinach
- 2 garlic cloves, minced
- 1 tablespoon olive oil
- Juice of ½ lime
- 1 tablespoon parsley, chopped

Directions:

1. In your slow cooker, mix the trout with the olives, spinach, and the other ingredients, toss, put the lid on and cook on Low for 3 hours.
2. Divide everything into bowls and serve.

per serving: 288 calories,30.8g protein, 2.9g carbohydrates, 16.7g fat, 1.3g fiber, 84mg cholesterol, 376mg sodium, 581mg potassium.

Calamari Curry with Coriander

Preparation time: 10 minutes
Cooking time: 3 hours
Servings: 4

Ingredients:

- 1 pound calamari rings
- ½ tablespoon yellow curry paste
- 1 cup of coconut milk
- ½ teaspoon turmeric powder
- ½ cup chicken stock
- 2 garlic cloves, minced
- ½ tablespoon coriander, chopped
- 2 tablespoons lemon juice

Directions:

1. In your slow cooker, mix the rings with the curry paste, coconut milk, and the other ingredients, toss, put the lid on and cook on High for 3 hours.
2. Divide the curry into bowls and serve.

per serving: 213 calories, 3.6g protein, 9.1g carbohydrates, 19.1g fat, 1.8g fiber, 0mg cholesterol, 157mg sodium, 183mg potassium.

Balsamic Trout with Cumin

Preparation time: 10 minutes
Cooking time: 3 hours
Servings: 4

Ingredients:

- 1 pound trout fillets, boneless
- ½ cup chicken stock
- 2 garlic cloves, minced
- 2 tablespoons balsamic vinegar
- ½ teaspoon cumin, ground
- 1 tablespoon parsley, chopped
- 1 tablespoon olive oil

Directions:

1. In your slow cooker, mix the trout with the stock, garlic, and the other ingredients, toss gently, put the lid on and cook on High for 3 hours.
2. Divide the mix between plates and serve.

per serving: 252 calories, 30.5g protein, 0.8g carbohydrates, 13.3g fat, 0.1g fiber, 84mg cholesterol, 173mg sodium, 548mg potassium.

Oregano Shrimp Bowls with Garlic

Preparation time: 10 minutes
Cooking time: 1 hour
Servings: 4

Ingredients:

- 1 pound shrimp, peeled and deveined
- ½ cup cherry tomatoes halved
- ½ cup baby spinach
- 1 tablespoon lime juice
- 1 tablespoon oregano, chopped
- ¼ cup fish stock
- ½ teaspoon sweet paprika
- 2 garlic cloves, chopped

Directions:

1. In your slow cooker, mix the shrimp with the cherry tomatoes, spinach, and the other ingredients, toss, put the lid on and cook on High for 1 hour.
2. Divide everything between plates and serve.

per serving: 161 calories,27.3g protein, 6.8g carbohydrates, 2.2g fat, 1.5g fiber, 239mg cholesterol, 312mg sodium, 413mg potassium.

Sweet Salmon Mix

Preparation time: 10 minutes
Cooking time: 2 hours
Servings: 4

Ingredients:

- 1 pound salmon fillets, boneless
- 1 cup strawberries, halved
- ½ cup of orange juice
- Zest of 1 lemon, grated
- 4 scallions, chopped
- 1 teaspoon balsamic vinegar
- 1 tablespoon chives, chopped

Directions:

1. In your slow cooker, mix the salmon with the strawberries, orange juice, and the other ingredients, toss, put the lid on and cook on High for 2 hours.
2. Divide everything into bowls and serve.

per serving: 181 calories,22.7g protein, 7.1g carbohydrates, 7.2g fat, 1.2g fiber, 50mg cholesterol, 53mg sodium, 597mg potassium.

Shrimps and Salmon Mix

Preparation time: 5 minutes
Cooking time: 1 hour and 30 minutes
Servings: 4

Ingredients:

- 1 pound shrimp, peeled and deveined
- ½ pound salmon fillets, boneless and cubed
- 1 cup cherry tomatoes, halved
- ½ cup chicken stock
- ½ teaspoon chili powder
- ½ teaspoon rosemary, dried
- 1 tablespoon parsley, chopped
- 2 tablespoons tomato sauce
- 2 garlic cloves, minced

Directions:

1. In your slow cooker, combine the shrimp with the salmon, tomatoes, and the other ingredients, toss gently, put the lid on, and cook on High for 1 hour and 30 minutes.
2. Divide the mix into bowls and serve.

per serving: 225 calories,37.6g protein, 4.8g carbohydrates, 5.7g fat, 0.9g fiber, 264mg cholesterol, 444mg sodium, 563mg potassium.

Chives Cod with Broccoli

Preparation time: 10 minutes
Cooking time: 3 hours
Servings: 4

Ingredients:

- 1-pound cod fillets
- 1 cup broccoli florets
- ½ cup vegetable stock
- 2 tablespoons tomato paste
- 2 garlic cloves, minced
- 1 red onion, minced
- ½ teaspoon rosemary, dried
- 1 tablespoon chives, chopped

Directions:

1. In your slow cooker, mix the cod with the broccoli, stock, tomato paste, and the other ingredients, toss, put the lid on and cook on Low for 3 hours.
2. Divide the mix between plates and serve.

per serving: 121 calories,21.6g protein, 6.7g carbohydrates, 1.2g fat, 1.8g fiber, 55mg cholesterol, 104mg sodium, 219mg potassium.

Cinnamon Trout with Cayenne Pepper

Preparation time: 5 minutes
Cooking time: 3 hours
Servings: 2

Ingredients:
- 1 pound trout fillets, boneless
- 1 tablespoon ground cinnamon
- ¼ cup chicken stock
- 2 tablespoons chili pepper, minced
- A pinch of cayenne pepper
- 1 tablespoon chives, chopped

Directions:
1. In your slow cooker, mix the trout with the cinnamon, stock, and the other ingredients, toss gently, put the lid on, and cook on Low for 3 hours.
2. Divide the mix between plates and serve with a side salad.

per serving: 449 calories,60.9g protein, 4.6g carbohydrates, 19.5g fat, 2.6g fiber, 168mg cholesterol, 250mg sodium, 1177mg potassium.

Seafood and Green Onions Mix

Preparation time: 10 minutes
Cooking time: 2 hours
Servings: 4

Ingredients:
- 1 green onions bunch, halved
- 10 tablespoons lemon juice
- 4 salmon fillets, boneless
- 2 tablespoons avocado oil

Directions:
1. Grease your Slow cooker with the oil, add salmon, top with onion, lemon juice, cover, cook on High for 2 hours, divide everything between plates and serve.

per serving: 255 calories,35g protein, 1.5g carbohydrates, 12.2g fat, 0.6g fiber, 78mg cholesterol, 87mg sodium, 763mg potassium.

Seafood Soup

Preparation time: 10 minutes
Cooking time: 8 hours and 30 minutes
Servings: 4

Ingredients:

- 2 cups of water
- ½ fennel bulb, chopped
- 2 sweet potatoes, cubed
- 1 yellow onion, chopped
- 2 bay leaves
- 1 tablespoon thyme, dried
- 1 celery rib, chopped
- 1 bottle clam juice
- 2 tablespoons tapioca powder
- 1 cup of coconut milk
- 1 pound salmon fillets, cubed
- 5 sea scallops, halved
- 24 shrimp, peeled and deveined
- ¼ cup parsley, chopped

Directions:

1. In your Slow cooker, mix water with fennel, potatoes, onion, bay leaves, thyme, celery, clam juice, and tapioca, stir, cover, and cook on Low for 8 hours.
2. Add salmon, coconut milk, scallops, shrimp, and parsley, cook on Low for 30 minutes more, ladle chowder into bowls, and serve.

per serving: 547 calories, 61.2g protein, 22.3g carbohydrates, 24.1g fat, 4.9g fiber, 340mg cholesterol, 475mg sodium, 1458mg potassium.

Shrimp and Cilantro Bowls

Preparation time: 5 minutes
Cooking time: 2 hours
Servings: 2

Ingredients:

- 1-pound shrimp, peeled and deveined
- ½ cup chicken stock
- 1 cup cauliflower florets
- ½ teaspoon turmeric powder
- ½ teaspoon coriander, ground
- ½ cup tomato passata
- 1 tablespoon cilantro, chopped

Directions:

1. In your slow cooker, mix the cauliflower with the stock, turmeric, and the other ingredients except for the shrimp, toss, put the lid on and cook on High for 1 hour.
2. Add the shrimp, toss, cook on High for 1 more hours, divide into bowls and serve.

per serving: 294 calories, 53.2g protein, 8.2g carbohydrates, 4.1g fat, 1.4g fiber, 478mg cholesterol, 760mg sodium, 554mg potassium.

Asian Style Salmon

Preparation time: 10 minutes
Cooking time: 3 hours
Servings: 2

Ingredients:
- 2 medium salmon fillets, boneless
- 2 tablespoons maple syrup
- 16 ounces mixed broccoli and cauliflower florets
- 2 tablespoons lemon juice
- 1 teaspoon sesame seeds

Directions:
1. Put the cauliflower and broccoli florets in your Slow cooker and top with salmon fillets.
2. In a bowl, mix maple syrup with lemon juice, whisk well, pour this over salmon fillets, sprinkle sesame seeds on top, and cook on Low for 3 hours.
3. Divide everything between plates and serve.

per serving: 273 calories,36.9g protein, 6g carbohydrates, 12g fat, 2.7g fiber, 12mg cholesterol, 112mg sodium, 1012mg potassium.

Garlic Shrimp Mix

Preparation time: 10 minutes
Cooking time: 1 hour and 30 minutes
Servings: 4

Ingredients:
- 2 tablespoons olive oil
- 1-pound shrimp, peeled and deveined
- ¼ cup chicken stock
- 1 tablespoon garlic, minced
- 2 tablespoons parsley, chopped
- Juice of ½ lemon

Directions:
1. Put the oil in your Slow cooker, add the stock, garlic, parsley, lemon juice, and whisk well.
2. Add shrimp, stir, cover, cook on High for 1 hour and 30 minutes, divide into bowls and serve.

per serving: 199 calories,26.1g protein, 2.6g carbohydrates, 9g fat, 0.1g fiber, 239mg cholesterol, 326mg sodium, 212mg potassium.

Steamed Fish

Preparation time: 10 minutes
Cooking time: 1 hour
Servings: 4

Ingredients:

- 2 tablespoons honey
- 4 salmon fillets, boneless
- 2 tablespoons soy sauce
- ¼ cup olive oil
- ¼ cup vegetable stock
- 1 small ginger piece, grated
- 6 garlic cloves, minced
- 2 tablespoons Worcestershire sauce
- 1 bunch leeks, chopped
- 1 bunch cilantro, chopped

Directions:

1. Put the oil in your slow cooker, add leeks, and top with the fish.
2. In a bowl, mix stock with ginger, honey, garlic, cilantro, and soy sauce, stir, add this over fish, cover and cook on High for 1 hour.
3. Divide fish between plates and serve with the sauce drizzled on top.

per serving: 397 calories,35.5g protein, 12.9g carbohydrates, 23.6g fat, 0.4g fiber, 78mg cholesterol, 624mg sodium, 761mg potassium.

Poached Cod

Preparation time: 10 minutes
Cooking time: 4 hours
Servings: 4

Ingredients:

- 1-pound cod, boneless
- 6 garlic cloves, minced
- 1 small ginger pieces, chopped
- ½ tablespoon black peppercorns
- 1 cup pineapple juice
- 1 cup pineapple, chopped
- ¼ cup white vinegar
- 4 jalapeno peppers, chopped

Directions:

1. Put the fish in your crock.
2. Add garlic, ginger, peppercorns, pineapple juice, pineapple chunks, vinegar, and jalapenos.
3. Stir gently, cover, and cook on Low for 4 hours.
4. Divide fish between plates, top with the pineapple mix, and serve.

per serving: 191 calories,26.9g protein, 16.6g carbohydrates, 1.4g fat, 1.6g fiber, 6.2mg cholesterol, 460mg sodium, 484mg potassium.

Ginger Catfish

Preparation time: 10 minutes
Cooking time: 6 hours
Servings: 4

Ingredients:

- 1 catfish, boneless and cut into 4 pieces
- 3 red chili peppers, chopped
- ½ cup of honey
- ¼ cup of water
- 1 tablespoon soy sauce
- 1 shallot, minced
- A small ginger piece, grated
- 1 tablespoon coriander, chopped

Directions:

1. Put catfish pieces in your Slow cooker.
2. Heat a pan with the coconut honey over medium-high heat and stir until it caramelizes.
3. Add soy sauce, shallot, ginger, water, and chili pepper, stir, pour over the fish, add coriander, cover and cook on Low for 6 hours.
4. Divide fish between plates and serve with the sauce from the slow cooker drizzled on top.

per serving: 184 calories, 4.4g protein, 37.7g carbohydrates, 2.9g fat, 0.4g fiber, 18mg cholesterol, 289mg sodium, 122mg potassium.

Lemon Trout with Spinach

Preparation time: 10 minutes
Cooking time: 2 hours
Servings: 4

Ingredients:

- 2 lemons, sliced
- ¼ cup chicken stock
- 2 tablespoons dill, chopped
- 12-ounce spinach
- 4 medium trout

Directions:

1. Put the stock in your Slow cooker, add the fish inside, top with lemon slices, dill, and spinach, cover, and cook on High for 2 hours.
2. Divide fish, lemon, and spinach between plates and drizzle some of the juice from the slow cooker all over.

per serving: 150 calories, 19.6g protein, 6.7g carbohydrates, 5.8g fat, 2.9g fiber, 46mg cholesterol, 160mg sodium, 8 2 54mg potassium.

Tuna Mix

Preparation time: 10 minutes
Cooking time: 4 hours and 10 minutes
Servings: 6

Ingredients:
- ½ pound tuna loin, cubed
- 1 garlic clove, minced
- 4 jalapeno peppers, chopped
- 1 cup olive oil
- 3 red chili peppers, chopped
- 2 teaspoons black peppercorns, ground

Directions:
1. Put the oil in your Slow cooker, add chili peppers, jalapenos, peppercorns,
2. and garlic, whisk, cover, and cook on Low for 4 hours.
3. Add tuna, stir again, cook on High for 10 minutes more, divide between plates, and serve.

per serving: 366 calories,10.3g protein, 1.5g carbohydrates, 36.8g fat, 0.7g fiber, 12mg cholesterol, 265mg sodium, 170mg potassium.

Bok Choy Sea Bass

Preparation time: 10 minutes
Cooking time: 1 hour and 30 minutes
Servings: 4

Ingredients:
- 1-pound sea bass
- 2 scallion stalks, chopped
- 1 small ginger piece, grated
- 1 tablespoon soy sauce
- 2 cups coconut cream
- 4 bok choy stalks, chopped
- 3 jalapeno peppers, chopped

Directions:
1. Put the cream in your Slow cooker, add ginger, soy sauce, scallions, jalapenos, stir, top with the fish and bok choy, cover, and cook on High for 1 hour and 30 minutes.
2. Divide the fish mix between plates and serve.

per serving: 427 calories,30.3g protein, 8.6g carbohydrates, 31.7g fat, 3.4g fiber, 60mg cholesterol, 628mg sodium, 784mg potassium.

Onion Cod Fillets

Preparation time: 10 minutes
Cooking time: 2 hours
Servings: 4

Ingredients:

- 4 medium cod fillets, boneless
- ¼ teaspoon nutmeg, ground
- 1 teaspoon ginger, grated
- 1 teaspoon onion powder
- ¼ teaspoon sweet paprika
- 1 teaspoon cayenne pepper
- ½ teaspoon ground cinnamon

Directions:

1. In a bowl, mix cod fillets with nutmeg, ginger, onion powder, paprika, cayenne pepper, and cinnamon, toss, transfer to your Slow cooker, cover and cook on Low for 2 hours.
2. Divide between plates and serve with a side salad.

per serving: 97 calories, 20.2g protein, 1.4g carbohydrates, 1.2g fat, 0.4g fiber, 40mg cholesterol, 81mg sodium, 26mg potassium.

Red Chard and Shrimps Bowls

Preparation time: 5 minutes
Cooking time: 1 hour
Servings: 2

Ingredients:

- 1-pound shrimp, peeled and deveined
- Juice of 1 lime
- 1 cup red chard, torn
- ½ cup tomato sauce
- 2 garlic cloves, minced
- 1 red onion, sliced
- 1 tablespoon olive oil
- ½ teaspoon sweet paprika
- 1 tablespoon parsley, chopped

Directions:

1. In your slow cooker, mix the shrimp with the lime juice, chard, and the other ingredients, toss, put the lid on and cook on High for 1 hour.
2. Divide the mix into bowls and serve.

per serving: 377 calories, 54g protein, 14.2g carbohydrates, 11.1g fat, 2.7g fiber, 478mg cholesterol, 930mg sodium, 702mg potassium.

Seafood and Baby Carrots Mix

Preparation time: 10 minutes
Cooking time: 4 hours and 30 minutes
Servings: 2

Ingredients:

- 1 small yellow onion, chopped
- 15 baby carrots
- 2 garlic cloves, minced
- 1 small green bell pepper, chopped
- 8 ounces of coconut milk
- 3 tablespoons tomato paste
- ½ teaspoon red pepper, crushed
- ¾ tablespoons curry powder
- ¾ tablespoon almond flour
- 1-pound shrimp, peeled and deveined

Directions:

1. In your food processor, mix the onion with garlic, bell pepper, tomato paste, coconut milk, red pepper, and curry powder, blend well, add to your Slow cooker, also add baby carrots, stir, cover, and cook on Low for 4 hours.
2. Add tapioca and shrimp, stir, cover, and cook on Low for 30 minutes more.
3. Divide into bowls and serve.

per serving: 315 calories,28.8g protein, 14.9g carbohydrates, 16.3g fat, 3.8g fiber, 239mg cholesterol, 328mg sodium, 639mg potassium.

Indian Shrimp with Coriander and Turmeric

Preparation time: 5 minutes
Cooking time: 1 hour
Servings: 2

Ingredients:
- 4 scallions, chopped
- 1 tablespoon olive oil
- 1 pound shrimp, peeled and deveined
- ½ teaspoon garam masala
- ½ teaspoon coriander, ground
- ½ teaspoon turmeric powder
- 1 tablespoon lime juice
- ½ cup chicken stock
- ¼ cup lime leaves, torn

Directions:
1. In your slow cooker, mix the shrimp with the oil, scallions, masala, and the other ingredients, toss, put the lid on and cook on High for 1 hour.
2. Divide the mix into bowls and serve.

per serving: 344 calories,52.4g protein, 6.2g carbohydrates, 11.1g fat, 0.9g fiber, 478mg cholesterol, 750mg sodium, 485mg potassium.

Beef

Beef and Zucchinis Bowls

Preparation time: 10 minutes
Cooking time: 8 hours
Servings: 4

Ingredients:

- 1 pound beef loin, cut into strips
- 1 tablespoon olive oil
- ¼ cup beef stock
- ½ teaspoon sweet paprika
- ½ teaspoon chili powder
- 2 small zucchinis, cubed
- 1 tablespoon balsamic vinegar
- 1 tablespoon chives, chopped

Directions:

1. In your slow cooker, mix the beef with the oil, stock, and the other ingredients, toss, put the lid on and cook on Low for 8 hours.
2. Divide the mix between plates and serve.

per serving: 250 calories,31.1g protein, 2.4g carbohydrates, 13.2g fat, 0.9g fiber, 81mg cholesterol, 121mg sodium, 566mg potassium.

Juice Beef with Garlic

Preparation time: 10 minutes
Cooking time: 10 hours
Servings: 8

Ingredients:

- 3-pound beef tenderloin
- 1 fennel bulb, cut into wedges
- 2 yellow onions, cut into wedges
- 1 cup carrot, sliced
- 14 ounces canned tomatoes, chopped
- 1 cup grape juice, fresh
- 2 tablespoons tapioca, crushed
- 2 tablespoons tomato paste
- 1 teaspoon rosemary, dried
- 4 garlic cloves, minced

Directions:

1. In your Slow cooker, mix beef with fennel, onions, carrots, tomatoes, juice, tapioca, tomato paste, rosemary, and garlic, cover, and cook on Low for 10 hours.
2. Divide everything between plates and serve.

per serving: 411 calories,50.9g protein, 14.2g carbohydrates, 15.8g fat, 2.7g fiber, 156mg cholesterol, 133mg sodium, 1026mg potassium.

Onion Beef with Olives

Preparation time: 10 minutes
Cooking time: 8 hours
Servings: 4

Ingredients:

- 1 pound beef tenderloin, sliced
- ½ cup tomato passata
- 1 red onion, sliced
- 1 cup kalamata olives, pitted and halved
- Juice of ½ lime
- ¼ cup beef stock
- 1 tablespoon chives, hopped

Directions:

1. In your slow cooker, mix the beef slices with the passata, onion, olives, and the other ingredients, toss, put the lid on and cook on Low for 8 hours.
2. Divide the mix between plates and serve.

per serving: 288 calories,33.8g protein, 5.5g carbohydrates, 14g fat, 1.7g fiber, 104mg cholesterol, 410mg sodium, 458mg potassium.

Beef Mix

Preparation time: 10 minutes
Cooking time: 8 hours
Servings: 4

Ingredients:

- 1 pound beef loin, boneless and roughly cubed
- 3 tablespoons honey
- ½ tablespoons oregano, dried
- 1 tablespoon garlic, minced
- 1 tablespoon olive oil
- ½ cup beef stock
- ½ teaspoon sweet paprika

Directions:

1. In your slow cooker, mix the beef loin with the honey, and the other ingredients, toss, put the lid on and cook on Low for 8 hours.
2. Divide everything between plates and serve.

per serving: 292 calories,31g protein, 14.2g carbohydrates, 13.1g fat, 0.4g fiber, 81mg cholesterol, 161mg sodium, 434mg potassium.

Beef with Yogurt Sauce

Preparation time: 10 minutes
Cooking time: 8 hours
Servings: 4

Ingredients:

- 1 pound beef loin, cubed
- 1 teaspoon garam masala
- ½ teaspoon turmeric powder
- 1 cup beef stock
- 1 teaspoon garlic, minced
- ½ cup Greek-style yogurt
- 1 tablespoon chives, chopped

Directions:

1. In your slow cooker, mix the beef with the turmeric, garam masala, and the other ingredients, toss, put the lid on and cook on Low for 8 hours.
2. Divide everything into bowls and serve.

per serving: 228 calories,33.8g protein, 1.5g carbohydrates, 9.6g fat, 0.1g fiber, 82mg cholesterol, 269mg sodium, 469mg potassium.

Beans Mix with Meat

Preparation time: 10 minutes
Cooking time: 8 hours
Servings: 4

Ingredients:

- 1 red bell pepper, chopped
- 1 pound beef loin, cubed
- 1 tablespoon olive oil
- 1 cup canned black beans, drained and rinsed
- ½ cup tomato sauce
- 1 yellow onion, chopped
- 1 teaspoon Italian seasoning
- 1 tablespoon oregano, chopped

Directions:

1. In your slow cooker, mix the beef with the bell pepper, oil, and the other ingredients, toss, put the lid on and cook on Low for 8 hours.
2. Divide the mix between plates and serve.

per serving: 437 calories,41.9g protein, 37.6g carbohydrates, 14.3g fat, 9.3g fiber, 81mg cholesterol, 228mg sodium, 1322mg potassium.

Beef and Spinach Bowls

Preparation time: 10 minutes
Cooking time: 7 hours
Servings: 4

Ingredients:

- 1 red onion, sliced
- 1-pound beef loin, cubed
- 1 cup tomato passata
- 1 cup baby spinach
- 1 teaspoon olive oil
- ½ cup beef stock
- 1 tablespoon basil, chopped

Directions:

1. In your slow cooker, mix the beef with the onion, passata, and the other ingredients except for the spinach, toss, put the lid on and cook on Low for 6 hours and 30 minutes.
2. Add the spinach, toss, put the lid on, cook on Low for 30 minutes more, divide into bowls, and serve.

per serving: 246 calories,31.7g protein, 4.5g carbohydrates, 11.1g fat, 0.8g fiber, 81mg cholesterol, 94mg sodium, 470mg potassium.

Chilies Meat Mix

Preparation time: 10 minutes
Cooking time: 7 hours
Servings: 4

Ingredients:

- 1 pound beef loin, cubed
- 1 tablespoon olive oil
- ½ green bell pepper, chopped
- 1 red onion, sliced
- ½ red bell pepper, chopped
- 1 garlic clove, minced
- 2 ounces canned green chilies, chopped
- ½ cup tomato passata
- 1 tablespoon chili powder
- 1 tablespoon cilantro, chopped

Directions:

1. In your slow cooker, mix the beef with the oil, bell pepper, and the other ingredients, toss, put the lid on and cook on Low for 7 hours.
2. Divide into bowls and serve right away.

per serving: 263 calories,31.3g protein, 5.9g carbohydrates, 13.4g fat, 1.5g fiber, 81mg cholesterol, 83mg sodium, 494mg potassium.

Fragrant Tenderloin

Preparation time: 10 minutes
Cooking time: 8 hours
Servings: 2

Ingredients:

- 2 beef tenderloin
- ½ cup tomato juice, fresh
- 1 tablespoon balsamic vinegar
- 1 tablespoon mustard
- 1 tablespoon chives, chopped

Directions:

1. In your slow cooker, combine the meat with the tomato juice, and the other ingredients, toss, put the lid on, and cook on Low for 8 hours.
2. Divide between plates and serve with a side salad.

per serving: 214 calories,26.5g protein, 4.7g carbohydrates, 9.4g fat, 1.1g fiber, 78mg cholesterol, 214mg sodium, 491mg potassium.

Meat and Corn Mix

Preparation time: 10 minutes
Cooking time: 8 hours
Servings: 2

Ingredients:

- 2 teaspoons olive oil
- 3 scallions, chopped
- 1 pound beef loin, cubed
- 1 cup of corn kernels
- ½ cup Greek-style yogurt
- ½ cup beef stock
- 2 garlic cloves, minced
- 1 tablespoon pomegranate sauce
- 1 tablespoon parsley, chopped

Directions:

1. In your slow cooker, combine the beef with the corn, oil, scallions, and the other ingredients except for the yogurt, toss, put the lid on and cook on Low for 7 hours.
2. Add the yogurt, toss, cook on Low for 1 more hour, divide into bowls and serve.

per serving: 284 calories,32.8g protein, 10.2g carbohydrates, 13.3g fat, 1.5g fiber, 81mg cholesterol, 174mg sodium, 548mg potassium.

Lime Beef Mix

Preparation time: 10 minutes
Cooking time: 8 hours
Servings: 4

Ingredients:

- 1-pound beef loin, cubed
- 1 tablespoon olive oil
- 3 garlic cloves, minced
- ½ yellow onion, chopped
- ½ cup beef stock
- 1 tablespoon apple cider vinegar
- 1 tablespoon lime zest, grated

Directions:

1. In your slow cooker, mix the beef with the oil, garlic, and the other ingredients, toss, put the lid on, and cook on Low for 8 hours.
2. Divide everything between plates and serve.

per serving: 249 calories,31g protein, 2.3g carbohydrates, 13.1g fat, 0.5g fiber, 81mg cholesterol, 161mg sodium, 436mg potassium.

Coriander Beef Chops

Preparation time: 10 minutes
Cooking time: 6 hours
Servings: 4

Ingredients:

- ½ pound beef chops
- ¼ tablespoons olive oil
- 2 garlic clove, minced
- ¼ teaspoon chili powder
- ½ cup beef stock
- ½ teaspoon coriander, ground
- ¼ teaspoon mustard powder
- 1 tablespoon tarragon, chopped

Directions:

1. Grease your slow cooker with the oil and mix the beef chops with the garlic, stock, and the other ingredients inside.
2. Toss, put the lid on, cook on Low for 6 hours, divide between plates and serve with a side salad.

per serving: 204 calories,11.5g protein, 1.6g carbohydrates, 16.3g fat, 0.1g fiber, 44mg cholesterol, 456mg sodium, 41mg potassium.

Spicy Lime Beef Chops

Preparation time: 10 minutes
Cooking time: 5 hours
Servings: 4

Ingredients:

- 2 teaspoons avocado oil
- 1 pound beef chops, bone-in
- 2 tablespoons mayonnaise, low-fat
- ½ tablespoon honey
- ¼ cup beef stock
- ½ tablespoon lime juice

Directions:

1. In your slow cooker, mix the beef chops with the oil, honey, and the other ingredients, toss well, put the lid on, and cook on High for 5 hours.
2. Divide beef chops between plates and serve.

per serving: 253 calories,34.7g protein, 4.6g carbohydrates, 9.9g fat, 0.1g fiber, 103mg cholesterol, 177mg sodium, 480mg potassium.

Chives Turmeric Beef

Preparation time: 10 minutes
Cooking time: 5 hours
Servings: 4

Ingredients:

- 1 pound beef chops
- 2 teaspoons avocado oil
- 1 teaspoon turmeric powder
- ½ teaspoon sweet paprika
- 1 cup beef stock
- 1 red onion, sliced
- 1 tablespoon chives, chopped

Directions:

1. In your slow cooker, mix the beef chops with the oil, turmeric, and the other ingredients, toss, put the lid on and cook on High for 5 hours.
2. Divide everything between plates and serve.

per serving: 486 calories,38.8g protein, 15.5g carbohydrates, 29.6g fat, 3g fiber, 54mg cholesterol, 204mg sodium, 779mg potassium.

Chili and Garlic Beef

Preparation time: 10 minutes
Cooking time: 4 hours
Servings: 4

Ingredients:
- 1-pound beef chops
- 2 teaspoons avocado oil
- 2 scallions, chopped
- 1 green chili pepper, minced
- ½ teaspoon turmeric powder
- 1 teaspoon chili powder
- ½ cup vegetable stock
- 2 garlic cloves, minced

Directions:
1. In your slow cooker, mix the beef chops with the oil, scallions, and the other ingredients, toss, put the lid on and cook on High for 4 hours.
2. Divide everything between plates and serve.

per serving: 310 calories,23.3g protein, 2.8g carbohydrates, 21.8g fat, 0.9g fiber, 60mg cholesterol, 470mg sodium, 89mg potassium.

Beef Mix with Onions

Preparation time: 10 minutes
Cooking time: 7 hours
Servings: 4

Ingredients:
- 1-pound beef loin, cubed
- 2 teaspoons olive oil
- 2 red onions, sliced
- 1 cup Greek-style yogurt
- ¼ cup beef stock
- 1 teaspoon chili powder
- ½ teaspoon rosemary, dried
- 1 tablespoon parsley, chopped

Directions:
1. In your slow cooker, mix the beef with the onions, oil, and the other ingredients, toss, put the lid on and cook on low for 7 hours.
2. Divide everything between plates and serve.

per serving: 252 calories,31.2g protein, 5.7g carbohydrates, 12g fat, 1.5g fiber, 81mg cholesterol, 121mg sodium, 493mg potassium.

Beef and Okra Saute

Preparation time: 10 minutes
Cooking time: 6 hours
Servings: 4

Ingredients:

- 1 pound beef loin, cubed
- 1 cup okra, sliced
- 2 teaspoons olive oil
- 1 red onion, chopped
- ¼ cup beef stock
- ½ teaspoon chili powder
- ½ teaspoon turmeric powder
- 1 cup tomato passata

Directions:

1. In your slow cooker, combine the beef with the okra, oil, and the other ingredients, toss, put the lid on and cook on High for 6 hours.
2. Divide the mix between plates and serve.

per serving: 258 calories,31.7g protein, 6.4g carbohydrates, 12g fat, 1.6g fiber, 81mg cholesterol, 118mg sodium, 522mg potassium.

Chives Beef with Cumin

Preparation time: 10 minutes
Cooking time: 4 hours
Servings: 4

Ingredients:

- 1 pound beef chops
- ½ cup chives, chopped
- ½ cup tomato passata
- 2 scallions, chopped
- 2 teaspoons olive oil
- 2 garlic cloves, minced
- ½ teaspoon sweet paprika
- 1 teaspoon cumin, ground

Directions:

1. In your slow cooker, mix the beef chops with the chives, passata, and the other ingredients, toss, put the lid on and cook on High for 4 hours,
2. Divide the mix between plates and serve.

per serving: 334 calories,22.8g protein, 2.5g carbohydrates, 25.6g fat, 0.5g fiber, 85mg cholesterol, 58mg sodium, 60mg potassium.

Oregano Beef with Tomato Sauce

Preparation time: 10 minutes
Cooking time: 4 hours
Servings: 4

Ingredients:

- 1 pound beef loin, cubed
- 1 tablespoon olive oil
- 1 tablespoon balsamic vinegar
- ½ tablespoon lemon juice
- 1 tablespoon oregano, chopped
- ½ cup tomato sauce
- 1 red onion, chopped
- ½ teaspoon chili powder

Directions:

1. In your slow cooker, mix the beef with the oil, vinegar, lemon juice, and the other ingredients, toss, put the lid on and cook on High for 4 hours.
2. Divide the mix between plates and serve right away.

per serving: 260 calories, 31.2g protein, 5.2g carbohydrates, 13.3g fat, 1.7g fiber, 81mg cholesterol, 228mg sodium, 557mg potassium.

Beef and Green Beans Bowls

Preparation time: 10 minutes
Cooking time: 6 hours
Servings: 4

Ingredients:

- 1 pound beef loin, cubed
- 1 tablespoon balsamic vinegar
- 1 cup green beans, trimmed and halved
- 1 tablespoon lime juice
- 1 tablespoon avocado oil
- ½ teaspoon rosemary, dried
- 1 cup beef stock
- 1 tablespoon chives, chopped

Directions:

1. In your slow cooker, mix the beef loin with the green beans, vinegar, and the other ingredients, toss, put the lid on, and cook on Low for 6 hours.
2. Divide the mix between plates and serve.

per serving: 225 calories, 31.6g protein, 2.3g carbohydrates, 10.1g fat, 1.2g fiber, 81mg cholesterol, 230mg sodium, 493mg potassium.

Mint Meat Chops

Preparation time: 10 minutes
Cooking time: 4 hours
Servings: 5

Ingredients:
- 2 tablespoons olive oil
- 1 pound beef chops
- 1 tablespoon mint, chopped
- ½ teaspoon garam masala
- ½ cup coconut cream
- 1 red onion, chopped
- 2 tablespoons garlic, minced

Directions:
1. In your slow cooker, mix the beef chops with the oil, mint, and the other ingredients, toss, put the lid on and cook on High for 4 hours.
2. Divide the mix between plates and serve warm.

per serving: 360 calories,19g protein, 4.6g carbohydrates, 29.9g fat, 1.2g fiber, 68mg cholesterol, 128mg sodium, 127mg potassium.

Beef and Vegetable Plates

Preparation time: 10 minutes
Cooking time: 7 hours
Servings: 4

Ingredients:
- 1 tablespoon avocado oil
- 1 pound beef loin, cubed
- 2 scallions, chopped
- 1 cup artichoke hearts
- ½ teaspoon chili powder
- 1 cup tomato passata
- ¼ tablespoon dill, chopped

Directions:
1. In your slow cooker, combine the beef with the artichokes and the other ingredients, toss, put the lid on and cook on Low for 7 hours.
2. Divide the mix between plates and serve.

per serving: 230 calories,31.2g protein, 4.4g carbohydrates, 10g fat, 1g fiber, 81mg cholesterol, 167mg sodium, 430mg potassium.

Beef with Paprika and Sweet Potato

Preparation time: 10 minutes
Cooking time: 4 hours
Servings: 4

Ingredients:

- 1 pound beef loin, roughly cubed
- 2 sweet potatoes, peeled and cubed
- ½ cup beef stock
- ½ cup tomato sauce
- ½ teaspoon sweet paprika
- ½ teaspoon coriander, ground
- 1 tablespoon avocado oil
- 1 tablespoon balsamic vinegar
- 1 tablespoon cilantro, chopped

Directions:

1. In your slow cooker, mix the beef with the potatoes, stock, sauce, and the other ingredients toss, put the lid on and cook on High for 4 hours
2. Divide everything between plates and serve.

per serving: 266 calories,31.7g protein, 12.5g carbohydrates, 10.1g fat, 2.3g fiber, 81mg cholesterol, 324mg sodium, 829mg potassium.

Oregano and Basil Beef

Preparation time: 10 minutes
Cooking time: 4 hours
Servings: 4

Ingredients:

- 1 teaspoon olive oil
- 1 pound beef loin, cubed
- 1 cup cherry tomatoes, halved
- 1 tablespoon basil, chopped
- ½ teaspoon rosemary, dried
- 1 tablespoon oregano, chopped
- 1 cup beef stock
- ½ teaspoon sweet paprika
- 1 tablespoon parsley, chopped

Directions:

1. Grease the slow cooker with the oil and mix the beef with the tomatoes, basil, and the other ingredients inside.
2. Toss, put the lid on, cook on High for 4 hours, divide the mix between plates and serve.

per serving: 234 calories,31.6g protein, 2.8g carbohydrates, 11g fat, 1.2g fiber, 81mg cholesterol, 261mg sodium, 558mg potassium.

Tender Beef with Eggplants

Preparation time: 10 minutes
Cooking time: 7 hours
Servings: 4

Ingredients:

- 1 pound beef loin, cubed
- 1 eggplant, cubed
- 2 scallions, chopped
- 2 garlic cloves, minced
- ½ cup beef stock
- ¼ cup tomato sauce
- 1 teaspoon sweet paprika
- 1 tablespoon chives, chopped

Directions:

1. In your slow cooker, mix the beef loin with the scallions, eggplant, and the other ingredients, toss, put the lid on and cook on Low for 7 hours.
2. Divide the mix between plates and serve right away.

per serving: 247 calories,32.3g protein, 8.9g carbohydrates, 9.9g fat, 4.7g fiber, 81mg cholesterol, 244mg sodium, 756mg potassium.

Lemon Beef with Onions

Preparation time: 10 minutes
Cooking time: 7 hours
Servings: 4

Ingredients:

- 1 pound beef loin, cubed
- 1 red onion, sliced
- ½ cup tomato sauce
- 1 tablespoon balsamic vinegar
- 1 tablespoon lemon juice
- 1 tablespoon lemon zest, grated
- 1 teaspoon olive oil
- 3 garlic cloves, chopped
- 1 tablespoon chives, chopped

Directions:

1. In your slow cooker, mix the beef with the onion, tomato sauce, and the other ingredients, toss, put the lid on, and cook on Low for 7 hours.
2. Divide the mix between plates and serve right away.

per serving: 241 calories,31.3g protein, 5.4g carbohydrates, 10.8g fat, 1.2g fiber, 81mg cholesterol, 225mg sodium, 550mg potassium.

Rosemary Beef with Scallions

Preparation time: 10 minutes
Cooking time: 4 hours
Servings: 4

Ingredients:
- 1 pound beef chops
- 1 tablespoon olive oil
- 3 garlic cloves, minced
- 1 tablespoon rosemary, chopped
- 1 cup kalamata olives, pitted and halved
- 3 scallions, chopped
- 1 teaspoon turmeric powder
- 1 cup beef stock

Directions:
1. In your slow cooker, mix the beef chops with the oil, rosemary, and the other ingredients, toss, put the lid on and cook on High for 4 hours.
2. Divide the mix between plates and serve.

per serving: 386 calories, 23.5g protein, 4.6g carbohydrates, 30.5g fat, 1.9g fiber, 85mg cholesterol, 547mg sodium, 97mg potassium.

Nutmeg Beef

Preparation time: 10 minutes
Cooking time: 6 hours
Servings: 4

Ingredients:
- 1-pound beef loin, roughly cubed
- 1 cup butternut squash, peeled and cubed
- ½ teaspoon nutmeg, ground
- ½ teaspoon chili powder
- ½ teaspoon coriander, ground
- 2 teaspoons olive oil
- 1 cup beef stock
- 1 tablespoon cilantro, chopped

Directions:
1. In your slow cooker, mix the beef with the squash, nutmeg, and the other ingredients, toss, put the lid on and cook on Low for 6 hours.
2. Divide the mix between plates and serve.

per serving: 249 calories, 31.4g protein, 4.4g carbohydrates, 12.1g fat, 0.9g fiber, 81mg cholesterol, 263mg sodium, 549mg potassium.

Aromatic Fennel Beef

Preparation time: 10 minutes
Cooking time: 4 hours
Servings: 4

Ingredients:

- 1 pound beef loin, roughly cubed
- 1 fennel bulb, sliced
- 1 tablespoon lemon juice
- 1 teaspoon avocado oil
- ½ teaspoon coriander, ground
- 1 cup tomato passata
- 1 tablespoon cilantro, chopped

Directions:

1. In your slow cooker, combine the beef with the fennel, lemon juice, and the other ingredients, toss, put the lid on and cook on High for 4 hours.
2. Divide the mix between plates and serve.

per serving: 235 calories,31.5g protein, 6g carbohydrates, 9.8g fat, 1.9g fiber, 81mg cholesterol, 94mg sodium, 636mg potassium.

Creamy Beef with Turmeric

Preparation time: 10 minutes
Cooking time: 6 hours
Servings: 4

Ingredients:

- 2 pounds beef loin, cubed
- 1 cup Greek-style yogurt
- 1/3 cup beef stock
- 2 teaspoons avocado oil
- 1 teaspoon turmeric powder
- 1 red onion, sliced
- 1 tablespoon cilantro, chopped

Directions:

1. In your slow cooker, mix the beef with the stock, oil, and the other ingredients except for the greek style yogurt, toss, put the lid on, and cook on Low for 5 hours.
2. Add the cream, toss, cook on Low for 1 more hour, divide the mix into bowls and serve.

per serving: 470 calories,67g protein, 5.4g carbohydrates, 20.1g fat, 0.8g fiber, 166mg cholesterol, 216mg sodium, 918mg potassium.

Beef with Capers

Preparation time: 10 minutes
Cooking time: 7 hours
Servings: 4

Ingredients:

- 1-pound beef loin, cubed
- 1 tablespoon capers, drained
- 1 cup greek style yogurt
- ½ cup beef stock
- ½ tablespoon mustard
- 3 scallions, chopped
- 2 teaspoons avocado oil
- 1 teaspoon cumin, ground
- 1 tablespoon parsley, chopped

Directions:

1. In your slow cooker, mix the beef with capers, stock, and the other ingredients except for the yogurt, toss, put the lid on, and cook on Low for 6 hours.
2. Add the yogurt, toss, cook on Low for 1 more hour, divide the mix between plates and serve.

per serving: 258 calories,32.4g protein, 4.9g carbohydrates, 12.3g fat, 0.8g fiber, 81mg cholesterol, 237mg sodium, 460mg potassium.

Masala Beef

Preparation time: 10 minutes
Cooking time: 7 hours
Servings: 4

Ingredients:

- 1 pound beef loin, cubed
- 1 teaspoon garam masala
- 1 tablespoon olive oil
- 1 tablespoon lime zest, grated
- 1 tablespoon lime juice
- ½ teaspoon sweet paprika
- ½ teaspoon coriander, ground
- 1 cup beef stock

Directions:

1. In your slow cooker, mix the beef with the garam masala, oil, and the other ingredients, toss, put the lid on and cook on Low for 7 hours.
2. Divide the mix between plates and serve.

per serving: 244 calories,31.1g protein, 0.9g carbohydrates, 13.1g fat, 0.3g fiber, 81mg cholesterol, 260mg sodium, 432mg potassium.

Cabbage and Beef Saute

Preparation time: 10 minutes
Cooking time: 5 hours
Servings: 8

Ingredients:

- 2 pounds beef loin, cubed
- 1 cup red cabbage, shredded
- 1 cup beef stock
- 1 teaspoon avocado oil
- 1 teaspoon sweet paprika
- 2 tablespoons tomato paste
- 1 tablespoon cilantro, chopped

Directions:

1. In your slow cooker, mix the beef with the cabbage, stock, and the other ingredients, toss, put the lid on and cook on High for 5 hours.
2. Divide everything between plates and serve.

per serving: 216 calories, 31g protein, 1.5g carbohydrates, 9.7g fat, 0.5g fiber, 81mg cholesterol, 166mg sodium, 466mg potassium.

Tender Beef with Lentils

Preparation time: 10 minutes
Cooking time: 7 hours
Servings: 4

Ingredients:

- 1 pound beef loin, cubed
- 1 cup lentils, drained and rinsed, cooked
- 1 tablespoon olive oil
- 1 yellow onion, chopped
- ¼ cup tomato sauce
- ¼ cup beef stock
- 1 tablespoon cilantro, chopped

Directions:

1. In your slow cooker, mix the beef with the lentils, oil, onion, and the other ingredients, toss, put the lid on and cook on Low for 7 hours.
2. Divide the mix between plates and serve.

per serving: 423 calories, 44.3g protein, 32.3g carbohydrates, 13.6g fat, 15.5g fiber, 81mg cholesterol, 196mg sodium, 944mg potassium.

Coriander Beef Mix

Preparation time: 10 minutes
Cooking time: 7 hours
Servings: 4

Ingredients:

- 1 pound beef loin, cubed
- 2 teaspoons avocado oil
- 1 tablespoon balsamic vinegar
- ½ teaspoon coriander, ground
- 1 cup beef stock

Directions:

1. In your slow cooker, mix the beef with the oil, vinegar, and the other ingredients, toss, put the lid on and cook on Low for 7 hours.
2. Divide the mix between plates and serve with a side salad.

per serving: 214 calories,31g protein, 0.2g carbohydrates, 9.9g fat, 0.1g fiber, 81mg cholesterol, 258mg sodium, 428mg potassium.

Beef and Endives Bowls

Preparation time: 10 minutes
Cooking time: 7 hours
Servings: 4

Ingredients:

- 1 pound beef loin, cubed
- 2 teaspoons avocado oil
- 2 endives, shredded
- ½ cup beef stock
- ½ teaspoon sweet paprika
- ¼ cup tomato passata
- 3 garlic cloves, minced
- 1 tablespoon chives, chopped

Directions:

1. In your slow cooker, mix the meat with the oil, endives, and the other ingredients, toss, put the lid on and cook on Low for 7 hours.
2. Divide the mix between plates and serve.

per serving: 261 calories,34.2g protein, 10g carbohydrates, 10.4g fat, 8.2g fiber, 81mg cholesterol, 217mg sodium, 1232mg potassium.

Beef and Lime

Preparation time: 10 minutes
Cooking time: 4 hours
Servings: 4

Ingredients:

- 1 pound beef loin, roughly cubed
- 2 small zucchinis, cubed
- Juice of 1 lime
- ½ teaspoon rosemary, dried
- 2 tablespoons avocado oil
- 1 red onion, chopped
- ½ cup beef stock
- 1 tablespoon garlic, minced
- 1 tablespoon cilantro, chopped

Directions:

1. In your slow cooker, mix the beef with the zucchinis, lime juice, and the other ingredients, toss, put the lid on and cook on High for 4 hours.
2. Divide the mix between plates and serve.

per serving: 242 calories, 31.9g protein, 5.8g carbohydrates, 10.6g fat, 1.7g fiber, 81mg cholesterol, 168mg sodium, 630mg potassium.

Beef Curry with Mustard

Preparation time: 10 minutes
Cooking time: 8 hours
Servings: 8

Ingredients:

- 2 pounds beef steak, cubed
- 2 tablespoons olive oil
- 3 potatoes, diced
- 1 tablespoon mustard
- 2 ½ tablespoons curry powder
- 2 yellow onions, chopped
- 2 garlic cloves, minced
- 10 ounces of coconut milk
- 2 tablespoons tomato sauce

Directions:

1. In your Slow cooker, mix oil with steak, potatoes, mustard, curry powder, garlic, coconut milk, tomato sauce, and pepper, toss, cover, and cook on Low for 8 hours.
2. Stir curry one more time, divide into bowls and serve.

per serving: 403 calories, 37.6g protein, 19.2g carbohydrates, 19.8g fat, 4.2g fiber, 101mg cholesterol, 107mg sodium, 971mg potassium.

Beef Tenderloin with Thyme Sprigs

Preparation time: 10 minutes
Cooking time: 8 hours and 30 minutes
Servings: 6

Ingredients:
- 4 pounds beef tenderloin
- 1 cup vegetable stock
- 1 tablespoon coconut oil
- 1 bay leaf
- 10 thyme sprigs
- 4 garlic cloves, minced
- 1 carrot, roughly chopped
- 1 yellow onion, roughly chopped
- 2 celery ribs, roughly chopped
- 1 cauliflower head, florets separated

Directions:
1. Heat a pan with the oil over medium-high heat, add beef tenderloin, brown for 5 minutes on each side, transfer to your slow cooker, add thyme springs, stock, bay leaf, garlic, celery, onion, and carrot, cover, and cook on Low for 8 hours.
2. Add cauliflower, cover slow cooker again, cook on High for 20 minutes more, divide everything between plates and serve.

per serving: 673 calories,89.1g protein, 6.8g carbohydrates, 30g fat, 2.2g fiber, 278mg cholesterol, 234mg sodium, 1337mg potassium.

Beef Tenderloin with Onions

Preparation time: 10 minutes
Cooking time: 8 hours
Servings: 8

Ingredients:
- 2 ½ pounds beef tenderloin
- 2 cups carrots, chopped
- 1 tablespoon olive oil
- 2 cup yellow onion, chopped
- 1 cup celery, chopped
- 1/3 cup German mustard
- ¼ teaspoon cloves, ground
- 2 tablespoons almond flour
- 2 bay leaves
- 2 tablespoons beef stock

Directions:
1. In your Slow cooker, mix beef with carrots, oil, onion, celery, pickle, mustard, cloves, flour, bay leaves, and stock, toss well, cover, and cook on Low for 8 hours.
2. Slice roast, divide between plates, drizzle cooking juices all over, and serve.

per serving: 351 calories,42.7g protein, 6.8g carbohydrates, 15.9g fat, 2.1g fiber, 130mg cholesterol, 126mg sodium, 671mg potassium.

Desserts

Honey and Cinnamon Apples

Preparation time: 10 minutes
Cooking time: 2 hours
Servings: 2

Ingredients:

- 2 tablespoons honey
- 1 tablespoon ground cinnamon
- 2 tablespoons walnuts, chopped
- A pinch of nutmeg, ground
- ½ tablespoon lemon juice
- ¼ cup of water
- 2 apples, cored and tops cut off

Directions:

1. In your slow cooker, mix the apples with the honey, cinnamon, and the other ingredients, toss, put the lid on and cook on High for 2 hours.
2. Divide the mix between plates and serve.

per serving: 237 calories,2.7g protein, 51.7g carbohydrates, 5.7g fat, 7.8g fiber, 0mg cholesterol, 5mg sodium, 310mg potassium.

Vanilla Pears with lime Juice

Preparation time: 10 minutes
Cooking time: 2 hours
Servings: 2

Ingredients:

- 2 tablespoons avocado oil
- 1 teaspoon vanilla extract
- 2 pears, cored and halved
- ½ tablespoon lime juice
- 1 tablespoon honey

Directions:

1. In your slow cooker combine the pears with the honey, oil, and the other ingredients, toss, put the lid on and cook on High for 2 hours.
2. Divide between plates and serve.

per serving: 179 calories,1g protein, 42.1g carbohydrates, 2.1g fat, 7.1g fiber, 0mg cholesterol, 5mg sodium, 301mg potassium.

Avocado and Almond Cake

Preparation time: 10 minutes
Cooking time: 2 hours
Servings: 4

Ingredients:
- ½ cup honey
- 2 tablespoons coconut oil, melted
- 1 cup avocado, peeled and mashed
- ½ teaspoon vanilla extract
- 1 egg
- ½ teaspoon baking powder
- 1 cup almond flour
- ¼ cup organic almond milk
- Cooking spray

Directions:
1. In a bowl, mix the honey with the oil, avocado, and the other ingredients except for the cooking spray and whisk well.
2. Grease your slow cooker with cooking spray, add the cake batter, spread, put the lid on, and cook on High for 2 hours.
3. Leave the cake to cool down, slice, and serve.

per serving: 322 calories, 3.8g protein, 40.1g carbohydrates, 18.7g fat, 3.4g fiber, 41mg cholesterol, 32mg sodium, 282mg potassium.

Tender Coconut Cream

Preparation time: 10 minutes
Cooking time: 1 hour
Servings: 2

Ingredients:
- 2 ounces coconut cream
- 1 cup of coconut milk
- ½ teaspoon almond extract
- 2 tablespoons honey

Directions:
1. In your slow cooker, mix the cream with the milk and the other ingredients, whisk, put the lid on, cook on High for 1 hour, divide into bowls, and serve cold.

per serving: 219 calories, 1.9g protein, 13.5g carbohydrates, 19.1g fat, 1.4g fiber, 0mg cholesterol, 9mg sodium, 167mg potassium.

Cinnamon Rice Pudding

Preparation time: 10 minutes
Cooking time: 1 hour
Servings: 4

Ingredients:
- 2 tablespoons almonds, chopped
- 1 cup of brown rice
- 2 cups organic almond milk
- 1 tablespoon honey
- ¼ teaspoon ground cinnamon
- ¼ teaspoon ginger, grated

Directions:
1. In your slow cooker, mix the coconut milk with the rice, honey, and the other ingredients, toss, put the lid on and cook on High for 1 hour.
2. Divide the pudding into bowls and serve cold

per serving: 482 calories,7g protein, 48g carbohydrates, 31.4g fat, 4.7g fiber, 0mg cholesterol, 20mg sodium, 469mg potassium.

Sweet Berry Bowls

Preparation time: 10 minutes
Cooking time: 1 hour
Servings: 4

Ingredients:
- 1 cup cherries, pitted
- 1 tablespoon honey
- ½ cup red cherry juice
- 2 tablespoons maple syrup

Directions:
1. In your slow cooker, mix the cherries with the honey and the other ingredients, toss gently, put the lid on, cook on High for 1 hour, divide into bowls and serve.

per serving: 80 calories,0.5g protein, 19.4g carbohydrates, 0g fat, 0.8g fiber, 0mg cholesterol, 5mg sodium, 23mg potassium.

Tender Cream

Preparation time: 10 minutes
Cooking time: 2 hours
Servings: 2

Ingredients:

- 2 tablespoons cashews, chopped
- 1 cup of coconut milk
- ½ cup blueberries
- ½ cup maple syrup
- ½ tablespoon coconut oil, melted

Directions:

1. In your slow cooker, mix the coconut milk with the berries and the other ingredients, whisk, put the lid on and cook on Low for 2 hours.
2. Divide the mix into bowls and serve cold.

per serving: 581 calories, 4.4g protein, 67.5g carbohydrates, 36.3g fat, 3.8g fiber, 0mg cholesterol, 27mg sodium, 553mg potassium.

Delightful Pudding

Preparation time: 10 minutes
Cooking time: 1 hour
Servings: 4

Ingredients:

- ¼ cup cashew butter
- 1 tablespoon coconut oil, melted
- ½ cup of brown rice
- 1 cup organic almond milk
- 2 tablespoons lemon juice
- ½ teaspoon lemon zest, grated
- 1 tablespoon honey

Directions:

1. In your slow cooker, mix the rice with the milk, coconut oil, and the other ingredients, whisk, put the lid on and cook on High for 1 hour.
2. Divide into bowls and serve.

per serving: 365 calories, 6.1g protein, 30.4g carbohydrates, 26.3g fat, 2.5g fiber, 0mg cholesterol, 14mg sodium, 322mg potassium.

Chia and Citrus Pudding

Preparation time: 10 minutes
Cooking time: 1 hour
Servings: 4

Ingredients:

- 1 tablespoon chia seeds
- ½ cup organic organic organic almond milk
- ½ cup oranges, peeled and cut into segments
- 1 tablespoon honey
- ½ teaspoon ground cinnamon
- 1 tablespoon coconut oil, melted
- 2 tablespoons pecans, chopped

Directions:

1. In your slow cooker, mix the chia seeds with the organic almond milk, orange segments, and the other ingredients, toss, put the lid on and cook on High for 1 hour.
2. Divide the pudding into bowls and serve cold.

per serving: 209 calories, 2.9g protein, 12.8g carbohydrates, 17.8g fat, 4.6g fiber, 0mg cholesterol, 6mg sodium, 181mg potassium.

Creamy Berries

Preparation time: 10 minutes
Cooking time: 1 hour
Servings: 2

Ingredients:

- ½ teaspoon nutmeg, ground
- ½ teaspoon vanilla extract
- ½ cup blackberries
- ½ cup blueberries
- ¼ cup coconut cream
- 1 tablespoon honey
- 2 tablespoons walnuts, chopped

Directions:

1. In your slow cooker, combine the berries with the cream and the other ingredients, toss gently, put the lid on, cook on High for 1 hour, divide into bowls, and serve.

per serving: 191 calories, 3.4g protein, 20.2g carbohydrates, 13.3g fat, 4.1g fiber, 0mg cholesterol, 6mg sodium, 215mg potassium.

Fruit Compote

Preparation time: 10 minutes
Cooking time: 1 hour
Servings: 2

Ingredients:

- 1 pound apples, cored and cut into wedges
- ½ cup of water
- 1 tablespoon honey
- 1 teaspoon vanilla extract
- ½ teaspoon almond extract

Directions:

1. In your slow cooker, mix the apples with the water and the other ingredients, toss, put the lid on and cook on High for 1 hour.
2. Divide into bowls and serve cold.

per serving: 277 calories, 11.7g protein, 32.6g carbohydrates, 11.6g fat, 4.6g fiber, 123mg cholesterol, 99mg sodium, 454mg potassium.

Plums Saute

Preparation time: 10 minutes
Cooking time: 1 hour
Servings: 4

Ingredients:

- 1 pound plums, pitted and halved
- ½ teaspoon nutmeg, ground
- 1 cup of water
- 1 ½ tablespoon honey
- 1 tablespoon vanilla extract

Directions:

1. In your slow cooker, mix the plums with the water and the other ingredients, toss gently, put the lid on, and cook on High for 1 hour.
2. Divide the mix into bowls and serve.

per serving: 42 calories, 0.2g protein, 9g carbohydrates, 0.2g fat, 0.3g fiber, 0mg cholesterol, 2mg sodium, 36mg potassium.

Cinnamon Mix

Preparation time: 10 minutes
Cooking time: 2 hours
Servings: 2

Ingredients:
- 2 cups peaches, peeled and halved
- 3 tablespoons honey
- ½ teaspoon ground cinnamon
- ½ cup coconut cream
- 1 teaspoon vanilla extract

Directions:
1. In your slow cooker, mix the peaches with the honey and the other ingredients, toss, put the lid on and cook on High for 2 hours.
2. Divide the mix into bowls and serve.

per serving: 300 calories,2.9g protein, 44g carbohydrates, 14.7g fat, 4g fiber, 0mg cholesterol, 11mg sodium, 465mg potassium.

Strawberry and Lemon Zest Cake

Preparation time: 10 minutes
Cooking time: 1 hour
Servings: 2

Ingredients:
- ¼ cup coconut flour
- ¼ teaspoon baking soda
- 1 tablespoon honey
- ¼ cup strawberries, chopped
- ½ cup of coconut milk
- 1 teaspoon peanut butter
- ½ teaspoon lemon zest, grated
- ¼ teaspoon vanilla extract
- Cooking spray

Directions:
1. In a bowl, mix the coconut flour with the baking soda, honey, and the other ingredients except for the cooking spray and stir well.
2. Grease your slow cooker with the cooking spray, line it with parchment paper, pour the cake batter inside, put the lid on, and cook on High for 1 hour.
3. Leave the cake to cool down, slice, and serve.

per serving: 253 calories,4.2g protein, 24.1g carbohydrates, 17.2g fat, 7.9g fiber, 0mg cholesterol, 181mg sodium, 210mg potassium.

Ginger Mix

Preparation time: 10 minutes
Cooking time: 2 hours
Servings: 2

Ingredients:
- 2 pears, peeled and cored
- 1 cup apple juice
- ½ tablespoon honey
- 1 tablespoon ginger, grated

Directions:
1. In your slow cooker, mix the pears with the apple juice and the other ingredients, toss, put the lid on and cook on Low for 2 hours.
2. Divide the mix into bowls and serve warm.

per serving: 203 calories, 1.1g protein, 52.1g carbohydrates, 0.6g fat, 7.1g fiber, 0mg cholesterol, 9mg sodium, 406mg potassium.

Almond Flour Cookies

Preparation time: 10 minutes
Cooking time: 2 hours and 30 minutes
Servings: 5

Ingredients:
- 1 tablespoon coconut oil, melted
- 2 eggs, whisked
- ¼ cup honey
- ½ cup raisins
- ¼ cup organic almond milk
- ¼ teaspoon vanilla extract
- ¼ teaspoon baking powder
- 1 cup almond flour

Directions:
1. In a bowl, mix the eggs with the raisins, organic almond milk, and the other ingredients and whisk well.
2. Line your slow cooker with parchment paper, spread the cookie mix on the bottom of the pot, put the lid on, cook on Low for 2 hours and 30 minutes, leave aside to cool down, cut with a cookie cutter, and serve.

per serving: 306 calories, 7.8g protein, 31.2g carbohydrates, 18g fat, 3.2g fiber, 65mg cholesterol, 37mg sodium, 198mg potassium.

Lime and Berries Jam

Preparation time: 10 minutes
Cooking time: 4 hours
Servings: 2

Ingredients:

- 2 cups blueberries
- ½ cup of water
- ¼ pound honey
- Zest of 1 lime

Directions:

1. In your slow cooker, combine the berries with the water and the other ingredients, toss, put the lid on and cook on High for 4 hours.
2. Divide into small jars and serve cold.

per serving: 266 calories,1.3g protein, 70.4g carbohydrates, 0.5g fat, 3.6g fiber, 0mg cholesterol, 5mg sodium, 142mg potassium.

Orange and Chia Seeds Bowls

Preparation time: 10 minutes
Cooking time: 3 hours
Servings: 2

Ingredients:

- ½ pound oranges, peeled and cut into segments
- 1 cup coconut cream
- ½ tablespoon almonds, chopped
- 1 tablespoon chia seeds
- 1 tablespoon honey

Directions:

1. In your slow cooker, mix the oranges with the cream and the other ingredients, toss, put the lid on and cook on Low for 3 hours.
2. Divide into bowls and serve.

per serving: 439 calories,6.5g protein, 34.9g carbohydrates, 33.8g fat, 10.4g fiber, 0mg cholesterol, 21mg sodium, 595mg potassium.

Quinoa and Walnuts Pudding

Preparation time: 10 minutes
Cooking time: 2 hours
Servings: 4

Ingredients:

- 1 cup quinoa
- 2 cups organic almond milk
- ½ cup of honey
- ½ tablespoon walnuts, chopped
- ½ tablespoon almonds, chopped

Directions:

1. In your slow cooker, mix the quinoa with the milk and the other ingredients, toss, put the lid on and cook on High for 2 hours.
2. Divide the pudding into cups and serve.

per serving: 316 calories,7g protein, 63.5g carbohydrates, 5g fat, 3.7g fiber, 0mg cholesterol, 94mg sodium, 367mg potassium.

Chia and Avocado Pudding

Preparation time: 10 minutes
Cooking time: 3 hours
Servings: 4

Ingredients:

- ½ cup almond flour
- 1 tablespoon lime juice
- 2 tablespoons chia seeds
- 1 cup avocado, peeled, pitted, and cubed
- 1 teaspoons baking powder
- ¼ teaspoon nutmeg, ground
- ¼ cup organic almond milk
- 2 tablespoons honey
- 1 egg, whisked
- 2 tablespoons coconut oil, melted
- Cooking spray

Directions:

1. Grease your slow cooker with the cooking spray and mix the chia seeds with the flour, avocado, and the other ingredients inside.
2. Put the lid on, cook on High for 3 hours, leave the pudding to cool down, divide into bowls and serve

per serving: 273 calories,4.4g protein, 17.6g carbohydrates, 22.6g fat, 5.7g fiber, 41mg cholesterol, 25mg sodium, 398mg potassium.

Cherries Pudding

Preparation time: 10 minutes
Cooking time: 3 hours
Servings: 4

Ingredients:

- ½ cup almonds, chopped
- ½ cup cherries pitted and halved
- ½ cup coconut cream
- ½ cup organic almond milk
- 1 tablespoon pumpkin puree
- 1 egg
- 2 tablespoons honey
- ½ cup almond flour
- ½ teaspoon baking powder
- Cooking spray

Directions:

1. Grease the slow cooker with the cooking spray and mix the almonds with the cherries, cream, and the other ingredients inside.
2. Put the lid on, cook on High for 3 hours, divide into bowls, and serve.

per serving: 221 calories,5.7g protein, 16.8g carbohydrates, 16.3g fat, 3.1g fiber, 41mg cholesterol, 36mg sodium, 296mg potassium.

Vanilla Cream

Preparation time: 10 minutes
Cooking time: 3 hours
Servings: 2

Ingredients:

- ¼ teaspoon ground cinnamon
- 1 cup peaches, pitted and chopped
- ¼ cup coconut cream
- Cooking spray
- 1 tablespoon maple syrup
- ½ teaspoons vanilla extract
- 2 tablespoons honey

Directions:

1. In a blender, mix the peaches with the cinnamon and the other ingredients except for the cooking spray and pulse well.
2. Grease the slow cooker with the cooking spray, pour the cream mix inside, put the lid on and cook on Low for 3 hours.
3. Divide the cream into bowls and serve cold.

per serving: 192 calories,1.5g protein, 33g carbohydrates, 7.4g fat, 2g fiber, 0mg cholesterol,6mg sodium, 256mg potassium.

Aromatic Plums

Preparation time: 10 minutes
Cooking time: 2 hours
Servings: 2

Ingredients:

- ½ pound plums pitted and halved
- 2 tablespoons honey
- 1 teaspoon cinnamon, ground
- ½ cup of orange juice

Directions:

1. In your slow cooker, mix the plums with the cinnamon and the other ingredients, toss, put the lid on and cook on Low for 2 hours.
2. Divide into bowls and serve as a dessert.

per serving: 102 calories,0.7g protein, 26.7g carbohydrates, 0.2g fat, 1g fiber, 0mg cholesterol, 1mg sodium, 166mg potassium.

Spicy Apples

Preparation time: 10 minutes
Cooking time: 2 hours
Servings: 2

Ingredients:

- 1 pound apples, cored and cut into wedges
- ½ cup organic almond milk
- ¼ teaspoon cardamom, ground
- 2 tablespoons honey

Directions:

1. In your slow cooker, mix the apples with the cardamom and the other ingredients, toss, put the lid on and cook on High for 2 hours.
2. Divide the mix into bowls and serve cold.

per serving: 138 calories,0.6g protein, 34.9g carbohydrates, 0.8g fat, 3.1g fiber, 0mg cholesterol, 39mg sodium, 178mg potassium.

Rhubarb Mix

Preparation time: 10 minutes
Cooking time: 2 hours
Servings: 2

Ingredients:

- 2 cups rhubarb, sliced
- ½ cup cherries pitted
- 1 tablespoon pumpkin puree
- ¼ cup coconut cream
- ½ cup of honey

Directions:

1. In your slow cooker, mix the rhubarb with the cherries and the other ingredients, toss, put the lid on and cook on High for 2 hours.
2. Divide the mix into bowls and serve cold.

per serving: 374 calories,2.5g protein, 82.4g carbohydrates, 7.5g fat, 3.9g fiber, 0mg cholesterol, 13mg sodium, 557mg potassium.

Peaches in Sauce

Preparation time: 10 minutes
Cooking time: 2 hours
Servings: 2

Ingredients:

- 3 tablespoons honey
- 1 pound peaches, pitted and cut into wedges
- ½ cup grape juice, fresh
- ½ teaspoon vanilla extract
- 1 teaspoon lemon zest, grated

Directions:

1. In your slow cooker, mix the peaches with the honey and the other ingredients, toss, put the lid on and cook on High for 2 hours.
2. Divide into bowls and serve.

per serving: 152 calories,1.1g protein, 38.8g carbohydrates, 0.3g fat, 1.3g fiber, 0mg cholesterol, 2mg sodium, 258mg potassium.

Apricot Cream

Preparation time: 10 minutes
Cooking time: 2 hours
Servings: 2

Ingredients:

- 1 cup apricots, pitted and chopped
- 1 cup peaches, pitted and chopped
- 1 cup coconut cream
- 3 tablespoons honey
- 1 teaspoon vanilla extract

Directions:

1. In a blender, mix the apricots with the peaches and the other ingredients, and pulse well.
2. Put the cream in the slow cooker, put the lid on, cook on High for 2 hours, divide into bowls, and serve.

per serving: 444 calories,4.5g protein, 48.4g carbohydrates, 29.3g fat, 5.4g fiber, 0mg cholesterol, 20mg sodium, 678mg potassium.

Grapes Mix

Preparation time: 10 minutes
Cooking time: 2 hours
Servings: 2

Ingredients:

- 1 cup grapes, halved
- ½ teaspoon vanilla extract
- 1 cup oranges, peeled and cut into segments
- ¼ cup of water
- 1 and ½ tablespoons honey
- 1 teaspoon lemon juice

Directions:

1. In your slow cooker, mix the grapes with the oranges, water, and the other ingredients, toss, put the lid on and cook on Low for 2 hours.
2. Divide into bowls and serve.

per serving: 125 calories,1.2g protein, 31.6g carbohydrates, 0.3g fat, 2.6g fiber, 0mg cholesterol, 3mg sodium, 264mg potassium.

Mango Bowls

Preparation time: 10 minutes
Cooking time: 3 hours
Servings: 2

Ingredients:

- 2 cups pomegranate seeds
- 1 cup mango, peeled and cubed
- ½ cup coconut cream
- 1 tablespoon lemon juice
- ½ teaspoon vanilla extract
- 2 tablespoons honey

Directions:

1. In your slow cooker, combine the mango with the pomegranate seeds and the other ingredients, toss, put the lid on and cook on Low for 3 hours.
2. Divide into bowls and serve cold.

per serving: 195 calories, 2.1g protein, 17.3g carbohydrates, 14.7g fat, 2.7g fiber, 0mg cholesterol, 11mg sodium, 307mg potassium.

Tangerine Cream

Preparation time: 10 minutes
Cooking time: 2 hours
Servings: 2

Ingredients:

- 1 tablespoon ginger, grated
- 3 tablespoons honey
- 3 tangerines, peeled and chopped
- 2 tablespoons agave nectar
- ½ cup coconut cream

Directions:

1. In your slow cooker, mix the ginger with the honey, mandarins, and the other ingredients, whisk, put the lid on and cook on High for 2 hours.
2. Blend the cream using an immersion blender, divide into bowls and serve cold.

per serving: 349 calories, 2.5g protein, 59.1g carbohydrates, 14.5g fat, 3.6g fiber, 0mg cholesterol, 17mg sodium, 376mg potassium.

Cranberries Sauce

Preparation time: 10 minutes
Cooking time: 1 hour
Servings: 4

Ingredients:

- 3 cups cranberries
- ½ cup of water
- ½ cup coconut cream
- ½ teaspoon vanilla extract
- ½ teaspoon almond extract
- ½ cup of honey

Directions:

1. In your slow cooker, mix the cranberries with the water, cream, and the other ingredients, whisk, put the lid on and cook on High for 1 hour.
2. Transfer to a blender, pulse well, divide into bowls and serve cold.

per serving: 244 calories,0.8g protein, 44.2g carbohydrates, 7.2g fat, 3.7g fiber, 0mg cholesterol, 7mg sodium, 242mg potassium.

Tender Pineapple

Preparation time: 10 minutes
Cooking time: 2 hours
Servings: 2

Ingredients:

- 2 cups pineapple, peeled and roughly cubed
- 1 ½ tablespoons peanut butter
- ½ cup coconut cream
- 2 tablespoons honey
- ½ teaspoon ground cinnamon
- ½ teaspoon ginger, grated

Directions:

1. In your slow cooker, mix the pineapple with the peanut butter, cream, and the other ingredients, toss, put the lid on and cook on High for 2 hours.
2. Divide into bowls and serve cold.

per serving: 357 calories,5.4g protein, 45.4g carbohydrates, 20.6g fat, 4.7g fiber, 0mg cholesterol, 67mg sodium, 435mg potassium.

Strawberry Mix

Preparation time: 10 minutes
Cooking time: 1 hour
Servings: 2

Ingredients:
- 2 tablespoons honey
- 1 cup orange segments
- 1 cup strawberries, halved
- A pinch of ginger powder
- ½ teaspoon vanilla extract
- ½ cup of orange juice
- 1 tablespoon chia seeds

Directions:
1. In your slow cooker, mix the oranges with the berries, ginger powder, and the other ingredients, toss, put the lid on and cook on High for 1 hour.
2. Divide into bowls and serve cold.

per serving: 365 calories,8g protein, 59g carbohydrates, 12.2g fat, 16.2g fiber, 0mg cholesterol, 12mg sodium, 123mg potassium.

Maple Plums Bowls

Preparation time: 10 minutes
Cooking time: 1 hour
Servings: 2

Ingredients:
- 2 teaspoons orange zest
- 1 tablespoon orange juice
- 1 cup plums, pitted and halved
- 1 cup mango, peeled and cubed
- 1 tablespoon maple syrup
- 3 tablespoons honey

Directions:
1. In your slow cooker, mix the plums with the mango and the other ingredients, toss, put the lid on and cook on High for 1 hour.
2. Divide into bowls and serve cold

per serving: 192 calories,1.1g protein, 50.3g carbohydrates, 0.5g fat, 2.1g fiber, 0mg cholesterol, 3mg sodium, 247mg potassium.

Cantaloupe Sauce

Preparation time: 5 minutes
Cooking time: 1 hour
Servings: 2

Ingredients:
- 2 cups cantaloupe, peeled and cubed
- 2 tablespoons honey
- 1 cup coconut cream
- 1 tablespoon pumpkin puree
- 1 tablespoon lemon zest, grated
- Juice of ½ lemon

Directions:
1. In your slow cooker, mix the cantaloupe with the honey, cream, and the other ingredients, toss, put the lid on and cook on High for 1 hour.
2. Blend using an immersion blender, divide into bowls and serve cold.

per serving: 397 calories, 4.3g protein, 37.9g carbohydrates, 29g fat, 4.5g fiber, 0mg cholesterol, 44mg sodium, 768mg potassium.

Lemon Confitur

Preparation time: 10 minutes
Cooking time: 3 hours
Servings: 2

Ingredients:
- ½ cup lemon juice
- 1 orange, peeled, and cut into segments
- 1 lemon, peeled and cut into segments
- ½ cup of water
- 2 tablespoons lemon zest, grated
- ¼ cup of honey
- A pinch of ground cinnamon

Directions:
1. In your slow cooker, mix the lemon juice with the honey, water, and the other ingredients, whisk, put the lid on and cook on Low for 3 hours.
2. Divide into small jars and serve cold.

per serving: 195 calories, 1.8g protein, 49.7g carbohydrates, 0.7g fat, 3.3g fiber, 0mg cholesterol, 16mg sodium, 305mg potassium.

Tender Pear Sauce

Preparation time: 10 minutes
Cooking time: 3 hours
Servings: 4

Ingredients:
- ½ pound pears, peeled and chopped
- ½ cup coconut cream
- ½ cup honey
- 1 tablespoon lemon zest, grated
- Juice of ½ lemon

Directions:
1. In your slow cooker, mix the pears with the cream and the other ingredients, whisk, put the lid on and cook on Low for 3 hours.
2. Blend using an immersion blender, divide into cups and serve cold.

per serving: 232 calories,1.1g protein, 45.5g carbohydrates, 7.2g fat, 2.6g fiber, 0mg cholesterol, 7mg sodium, 171mg potassium.

Semi-Sweet Rhubarb Jam

Preparation time: 10 minutes
Cooking time: 2 hours
Servings: 2

Ingredients:
- ½ pound rhubarb, sliced
- ¼ cup of honey
- 1 tablespoon lemon juice
- 1 cup of water

Directions:
1. In your slow cooker, mix the rhubarb with the honey and the other ingredients, toss, put the lid on and cook on High for 2 hours.
2. Whisk the jam, divide into bowls and serve cold.

per serving: 154 calories,1.2g protein, 40.2g carbohydrates, 0.3g fat, 2.2g fiber, 0mg cholesterol, 11mg sodium, 359mg potassium.

Fruit Marmalade

Preparation time: 10 minutes
Cooking time: 3 hours
Servings: 8

Ingredients:
- 1 cup apricots, chopped
- ½ cup of water
- 1 teaspoon vanilla extract
- 2 tablespoons lemon juice
- 1 teaspoon fruit pectin
- 2 cups of honey

Directions:
1. In your slow cooker, mix the apricots with the water, vanilla, and the other ingredients, whisk, put the lid on and cook on High for 3 hours.
2. Stir the marmalade, divide into bowls and serve cold.

per serving: 269 calories,0.5g protein, 72.1g carbohydrates, 0.2g fat, 0.6g fiber, 0mg cholesterol, 5mg sodium, 100mg potassium.

Apple and Avocado Bowls

Preparation time: 10 minutes
Cooking time: 2 hours
Servings: 5

Ingredients:
- 1 cup avocado, peeled, pitted, and cubed
- 1 cup mango, peeled and cubed
- 1 apple, cored and cubed
- 2 tablespoons honey
- 1 cup coconut cream
- 1 tablespoon lemon juice

Directions:
1. In your slow cooker, combine the avocado with the mango and the other ingredients, toss gently, put the lid on and cook on Low for 2 hours.
2. Divide the mix into bowls and serve.

per serving: 239 calories,2.1g protein, 23.3g carbohydrates, 17.4g fat, 4.7g fiber, 0mg cholesterol, 11mg sodium, 379mg potassium.

Made in the USA
Monee, IL
26 August 2023